THA[T]
SPECIAL

A SURVIVAL GUIDE TO TEACHING

10% GOES BACK TO LOCAL SCHOOLS

KICK ME

$y^2 = 36$

$4(3x+y) = 36$

$2x + 2x + 1b = 36$

$x + 1b = \frac{3}{6}$

-36

$x - 20 = 0$

DAN HENDERSON

outskirtspress
DENVER, COLORADO

7-17

Outskirts Press, Inc.
http://www.outskirtspress.com

ISBN: 978-1-4787-5245-5

Outskirts Press and the "OP" logo are trademarks belonging to Outskirts Press, Inc.

PRINTED IN THE UNITED STATES OF AMERICA

Disclaimer

All character names have been changed to maintain privacy. No personal information of the characters will ever be disclosed to any member of the public. All rights and materials are for the sole distribution by Glenhill Solutions Group LLC.

Table of Contents

Introduction

Scissors thrown as ninja stars; desks hurled in every direction. I began each day with yoga, limbering up my extremities to dodge projectiles. I signed up to be an educator, right? My principal downplayed children taking their clothes off during my interview to grab me and any warm body willing to teach in my inner-city school. I was handed a few textbooks and sent off feeling confident. During my first day, I was bitten by a first grader on the ankles and was realizing I just needed to survive. *That's Special* will give you practical tools to help you with teaching and child rearing while sharing humorous stories of kids pushing my buttons.

The end of my second day of teaching included twenty minutes of kids burping and falling out of chairs and pencils being flung at the whiteboard. I concluded that this meant war. I needed a better system. I needed to record everything to improve. I needed to laugh it off. Over my years of experience, I have been keeping a running journal to finally write a book for teachers that is as much entertaining as insightful.

My first years of teaching involved trying and often failing to lead a classroom effectively. My hope is that you laugh along the way and not take your teaching or parenting mistakes too seriously. As long as you learn from your errors, then you will continue to improve as a teacher or a parent.

Teachers choose to be educators to give back to the community, to be mentors, and let's be honest, to enjoy the summer vacation. The choice to be a teacher was not clear during the start of my career. After college I pursued a high paying job in finance. After long hours of repetitive administrative tasks, I was burned out. I volunteered across the globe, finally realizing my heart was to serve others. I came back to the United States with a renewed purpose.

My creative right brain and my interest in literature narrowed my choices to serve society as an educator, but I did not have the twenty thousand needed to go back to college. I joined an expedited trial-by-fire teaching program that let me earn a teaching certificate after one year of service in a poor part of the inner city. I was not prepared. Over time, I figured out how to adapt to teach all my students with all the growing pains along the way.

"Well, isn't that special," one my favorite lines from Dana Carvey's Church Lady on *Saturday Night Live*. When I saw my students doing something strange, I would think, *That's special*, as a cue to not take my job too seriously. It is my inspirational phrase and mantra for my mental health. To remind myself to get back in the saddle, laugh it off, and try again.

In fact, I found out I was socializing children just as much as teaching them. Life lessons you learned like not to interrupt someone who is presenting, saying thank you, or not picking your friend's nose even though your friend agreed. What is common social etiquette has to be taught somewhere; if it is not taught at home, then the responsibility falls on the teacher. Some children are exposed to social norms quicker than others. Children who have not accepted these social norms fall into another category, the special ones. As the special education teacher, my job is to discover how to teach those labeled "unteachable." However, just because some of these accounts are from my years as a special education teacher does not mean the effectiveness of these tools are limited to this setting. Parents, family members, and general education teachers will be emboldened to see the positive changes in their children's behavior after employing these tools.

I would ask any teacher or reader to humble his or her heart. To use these tools if your teaching needs to grow. Our society desperately needs more involved and fearless mentors. My push is to develop endurance in our youth, to have students rise to challenges and enjoy a lifelong love of learning.

This book is broken into short chapters that consist of two sections. The first section consists of the outrageous events that result in real-life improvisational comedy. Yes, these stories are based upon my real stories and all the extra life lessons we learn when teaching children. I narrate the story with the thoughts I had as the events unfolded.

All of the characters, including me, have been given new identities to protect the children. My true identity will never be known, as the world has gotten too serious. The students have been renamed as the "culprits."

I want to notify my readers that these children are not severely impaired. In fact, many of these culprits just need some extra interventions, discipline, and love. None of the children in this book have autism or more severe impairments. These children are the hell-raisers who would rather goof off than learn. These students believe they are superheroes, and society just can't quite figure these little ones out. The age range in this book is from pre-K to grade five, the early years of human development. As I socialized these children, along with teaching them, the following events unfolded.

Lastly, much of this book was written about my experiences working in inner-city schools somewhere in the United States. I am a male who has worked primarily as a special education teacher and who has worked as a special education coordinator. These tools will help you become a better teacher, parent, or caregiver. Please enjoy a brief synopsis of how the scenes were set and descriptions of a few of the characters!

Background:	Spider Man:
Spider Man rushes towards the closet, throwing imaginary Spider Man webs at his classmates. When asked to stop by the teacher, he looks in disbelief. "Without me, you would be dead by now." Spider Man was actually protecting his classmates. At least that's what his imagination tells him.	If Spider Man was twenty years older, doctors might put him in a special padded room. His pencil is a spaceship, his jumps are epic, and his words are that of a superhero. "I have come to save the day," he often says as he enters my classroom. I admire his imagination and his unyielding determination. He is only in special education because teachers do not want to respond to his imagination. In order to truly teach this child, I often repeat the old expression, "If you can't beat them, join them."

Background:	Mr. Chippendale:
Always trying to make the other students laugh, Mr. Chippendale interrupts the teacher by burping and saying offensive threats. This prompted the teacher to issue a series of warnings.	In this chapter, I call the culprit Mr. Chippendale. His threat is to take his clothes off. This student wants everyone's attention and will make threats when I push him to do work. To be quite frank, if I do not intervene in this child's life, he will grow up to be a jerk. Mr. Chippendale is constantly burping, interrupting others, and saying outrageous statements to get the whole class's attention. With the support of his mother, we see results, but only after the fateful day he stripped down to his skivvies.
Background:	**Monique:**
It is late spring, but a cold damp mist lies in the air. The children are growing weary of being indoors. The day is primed for an incident.	Monique has good intentions, but she cannot work well with others. An introvert who keeps to herself and is gifted in art, she is easily distracted if she is not learning about a topic that interests her. Most of all, she is curious, which gets her in trouble. This often leads to my patience being stretched, and I find myself rejecting her needs out of exhaustion.
Background:	**Gollum:**
Gollum is addicted to winning. Cold shoulders shrug when you ask him a question. Maybe he would listen to me if I were on a TV screen.	Dragging his shoulders, his eyes never look at you directly. His sole existence revolves around video games. He pouts, stomps, and yells to get his way. Gollum makes you realize how people can get addicted to gaming.

Background:	Chase AKA Michael Jackson:
Empathy for the wounded soul is apparent in the teachers' lounge. I see signs of crow's-feet forming; they're far too young to develop this sign of aging. I follow the teacher to her classroom to meet the culprit. The teacher frowns, clearly exhausted. "This is Chase. Have fun," she said sarcastically. I have just been introduced to Chase, the reincarnated King of Pop.	The universe has many mysteries yet to be solved. Dark matter, particle acceleration, and the skeleton structure of Chase. If he is forced to sit, his knees will somehow become bent on the seat and his whole body will lean forward on the desk. When he is sitting on the rug, and if my back is turned ever so slightly, I will turn back to discover Chase has invented a new yoga pose. When I create a visual sign in my attempt to indicate no talking, Chase will still talk. When a lesson is not adapted to Chase's kinetic nature, Chase impatiently adapts the lesson to his needs. Chase will dance, run, yell, burp, and be the first participant to call out in response to a question. Chase also has an affinity for grabbing his crotch instead of raising his hand and saying MJ's iconic sound, "Heee heee."

1

Michael Jackson Did More than Grab His Crotch

Chase has dance moves that stop pedestrians in their tracks. A crowd forms an energetic circle around Chase's street performances. Chase once showed me a YouTube video of him dancing that has over a thousand hits. On the outside, I have to keep my stern teacher face on during instruction. I cannot deny that the child's dance moves surpass my own. If Chase were twenty years older, I would want him as my dance instructor.

While he is only eight, he has already been introduced to some of the dance moves of Michael Jackson. His newfound love for the King of Pop has encouraged him to grab his crotch in the classroom. This is great for his YouTube popularity and his self-esteem. However, grabbing your crotch to answer a question sets up a very different scene than does raising your hand.

For the safety of others, the parents and teachers of our school decided that some of Chase's schooling would be completed in a small resource classroom with four other students. Resource classrooms are usually half the size of a regular classroom, and mine was formerly a dark, moldy closet. The problem with resource rooms is they often pile all the rebellious youth into one room. Chase has been granted an audience with full support for his mischief.

For one hour each day, I escort the culprits into the remolded closet. There are numbers on the floor indicating their mandatory spots. Mandatory seat assignments are necessary because the culprits do not always get along. They push each other discreetly so as to not summon the teacher's attention to inflict a consequence. Chase enters my room with a quick spin, landing on his number on the carpet with a big smile. Chase smiles at his peers to gain their approval.

I begin the math lesson with mischief in the air and hyper children. The group is only one hour away from recess on a beautiful fall day. The math lesson is on double-digit regrouping with addition. Remember having to carry the one to the tens place? Yes, it is a second-grade review of this standard. I call on Chase; he gets the answer right. To celebrate, he leaps up and tightly holds his appendage, saying the iconic MJ noise, "Heee heee!" The four other students begin to laugh hysterically.

"Chase, stop," I scold, but inwardly it is hard to keep my composure. I have to punish him for the inappropriate outburst. I give him a warning and remind him that I will not move his name forward on our behavior chart. The chart rewards positive behavior and only moves the student up if he or she is exhibiting positive actions. The class calms down, and we go over the next problem. This time, Chase grabs his package in an obvious act of defiance. The social acceptance is more valuable at the moment than any reward I can give.

With a firm grip on his nether regions, he starts singing "Just beat it, just beat it, nobody wants to be defeated."

The crotch grab of social acceptance pushes his puberty back a few years, but at the time it is well worth the social rewards. I wince at the sight of this display and have to get the classroom back in order.

"Chase, sit down!" I have to act fast and outwit this eight-year-old. I see endorphins rush to his head, as he is getting a thrill from performing. The same thrill he gets from performing to an anonymous crowd. At this point, the other students are rolling around on the ground and pleading for Chase to do it again. They are more interested in his entertainment than my math lesson.

I say, "Michael Jackson did more than grab his crotch. He had many moves, and if you do all your work this month, I will teach you his other moves." I can do a decent moonwalk, but that is the best move I can produce. If Chase can moonwalk, I will be out of luck to win their attention.

They look at me with disbelief, and I tell them I can moonwalk. "What's the moonwalk?" they question. My face sours as I realize how old I am in comparison with these eight-year-olds.

"The moonwalk is when you get on the tips of your toes and slide backward."

Fortunately, one child raises his hand, "I think I know another dance move by Michael Jackson."

"Yes, but I grew up with Michael Jackson, and I know all the moves," I have finally grabbed their attention by using what they like, and this is the perfect moment to exploit it. As a teacher, you can create incentives for younger students. However, it is far more effective to use the interests that a student is currently focused on. After all, don't we as adults work for incentives?

The next day, we are going over our phonics lesson. I say, "We blend sounds like *s* and *h* to make one sound like *sh*." We practice the sound with flashcards and make it into a game. We adapt the flashcards to create a game of Uno. One student forgets the cardinal rule of the game and forgets to say Uno when he has one card left.

Chase yells, "You did not say Uno! That means you have to take two cards." With ninja-like dexterity, he falls over a chair to hand the other player his cards, excited to be winning. I should have reminded the students about saying Uno. The other players are not amused, and the incident brings up an important teaching point.

If you want some specific actions from your students, take the time to explicitly explain the rules each day. For example, I should have told Chase he needs to stay in his chair and each student needs to call out Uno when only having one card left. The goal is to make sure to name the steps of the activity. Otherwise, they are children, and they will run wild.

Today, I forget to remind the students to not use inappropriate language.

The response from Chase is as follows: "I shit on my dog. I shit my pants. I shit on the couch," but spells his sentence on his personal whiteboard like this: "I sht an my dog. I sht mi pnts. I sht an the cuch."

"Chase! That is inappropriate," I scold as I check over his work at his desk. "If you do that again, you will not move forward on your behavior chart." The behavior system moves students up to the almighty color green and is set up so that after a fifteen-minute block, I move up the worthy participants. If I had been more explicit, I could have used the behavior plan by stating that you will not move up to green if you write words like *shit* on your paper. We review the rubric; Chase has a capital letter, period, and proper spacing and used a word with *sh*.

"OK, I am going to give you a three out of five. If you had not used a cuss word, I would have given you more credit."

He smiles and is about to jump to grab his crotch.

I shout loudly with annoyance, "No!" The whole room freezes, even Mr. Jackson.

With this child, repeated punishment has not worked. Taking away incentives has not worked. No one prepared me for a student who does not care about his recess being taken away. Nothing seems to work to control his behavior, and his teachers' weary looks indicate his daily battles are won. I have reached the end of my rope, and I do what any rational person does when being tested to the brink.

I take of my shoes and begin to moonwalk.

Chase exclaims, "How did you do that?"

Yes, I got him. *Thank you, Gerod, for teaching me how to moonwalk in college,* I think. "Let's do our schoolwork, and one day I might teach you." I have found my next incentive to motivate my difficult student.

After outsmarting an eight-year-old, I cheerfully think…*Heee, heee.*

Teaching Tool 1

Conduct a Student Survey

Why did I dance? To build a relationship. Never be unwilling to adapt as a teacher. This incident happened during my first year of teaching. Studies have shown learning is as unique as a person's fingerprint. Society needs to realize that some students will not fit a perfect mold. If the behavior is detrimental to learning, the teacher will need to correct the behavior but not before analyzing the motives behind the disruptions in the classroom.

The dancing was not the root of the problem. Chase wanted to feel successful and loved by his peers. Since he was struggling in school, he turned to dancing to feel wanted. Instead of shutting down the prospect of him dancing, I instead designated a time we would learn to dance together. The dancing became the incentive to learn, and the behavior in the classroom was eventually corrected.

Being the special education teacher allows me to experiment with different teaching techniques. Since the standard teaching techniques have not worked, I am hopefully left with more open-minded administration and parents. A team that realizes someone like Chase learns best when he moves and if he dances in the process, so what! When you show interest in a person, that person shows interest in you. I danced to build a relationship and create the incentive Chase wanted in return. Fortunately, most individuals desire a relationship, and if you tune in to your child's interest, you have won half the battle. When we take the time to know someone, that person wants to please us in return.

That day, I sacrificed a little order for the sake of showing the students my subpar dance moves. My students were shocked that I enjoyed having fun, and a bond was made during that session that forever changed my classroom. The students realized I knew something they were interested in, and on that common ground, we built a relationship. This made it easier for me to correct their behavior and dancing was an incentive I would use for the future.

The harder the school came down on Chase, the more he rebelled. The definition of insanity is repeating the same experiment and expecting different results. Instead of going insane, I tried a different system.

A week later, I created a chart that tracked my students' behavior, and we would only learn the moonwalk if the whole class earned a green smiley face on their behavior charts for four out of five days. That whole week, eyes were intent on their lessons, for the chance to learn to moonwalk. After four days of good behavior, they got their wish. I am not saying we did not have our incidents, but the simple things like crotch grabbing stopped.

Green means the students must keep their hands and feet to themselves and finish 80 percent of their work. You will have to determine the rigor in your classroom. I picked this Michael Jackson story for I changed my classroom culture after a realization my system was not working.

Many of these students have become culprits because they are not internally engaged. I adapt to their interests and use them as a reward. Remind them that the reward system that was put in place is for their benefit. A reward should be something they indicate they want as a reward. For example, one day, I showed my students a Michael Jackson video on the computer. This helped to show that I cared about their interests.

The younger the age, the more you will have to talk students through a situation and remind them you care about their well-being. Remember to enhance the relations you have with your students by rewarding them with their interests. If a student likes birds, have that child go to the library and check out as many books as possible on the subject. A simple way to find out if they like something is to give them a student survey.

There are plenty of simple student surveys online that you can use in your classroom. When I talk about surveys, I mean actual questions on paper or the computer that students fill out like a quiz. Make sure the survey lists how they like to work, independently or in a group. Include questions about how the students like to be rewarded and how they want to present their work.

Now that you have this information, you must adapt your teaching techniques to motivate your students. We, as logical thinkers, think once we do *a*, we must do *b*, and we will get the end result, *c*. We fail to realize that there might be a fundamental problem with *a*, and that may be why we are having difficulties executing a lesson targeted to get *c* results. When you seem to hit a wall with motivating or correcting behavior, reviewing the survey might remind you of better strategies for dealing with each student. When you reward a student with a desired incentive, you will be amazed at the correction in behavior.

You might need to get up and dance, if that is what motivates your class. If your students are producing results, that is what is important, and your pride takes a back seat. Give students just five minutes of joy a day and you may start to see a more manageable classroom. If you are a new teacher in the middle of the year, it is not too late to administer a student survey.

If you are a teacher or parent in middle school, dancing with you child may have the opposite effect. The older they are, the more responsibility teenagers crave. Slowly give them more trust, like, researching a topic on the computer. Give teens more creative expression in their work. Don't ignore their need for self-expression, as they are becoming young adults. This does not mean there are not rules or scoring rubrics for students to follow. All this means is that you are giving a child an incentive, and we all work for incentives.

My Survey: Typical Questions I Ask a Student the First Week of School

What are your hopes and dreams for the year?

What are your parents' hopes and dreams for you this year?

What is your favorite book?

Do you like to learn by moving, seeing, or hearing? (Give examples)

Can you describe how you think you would learn best?

What might make you angry in school?

What could you do to calm yourself down?

What subject do you need the most help in, reading or math?

What would you like to read this year?

How would you like to be rewarded? (Some examples: positive praise from the teacher, free choice, or researching a topic that interests you)

How often do you need breaks?

How should we monitor your growth in the classroom? (Some examples: presentations to the class, display your work, or private chart)

A kindergarten girl asked me this question after we had a talk about inappropriate touch:

When do I get to have a penis?

2
I Am Going to Take My Clothes Off

For all teachers, there will come a point when a student tests your resolve. In many instances, there is a lack of positive influences that has allowed a defiant bully to flourish. There have been threats, but without consequences, your threats mean nothing. No adult has executed the consequence to give the bully anything to fear. Parents who have legal responsibility over such a child know that humility is an unknown virtue. He or she will fight to be victorious. The child will sacrifice dignity if need be. Because the crying, screaming, and persistence has worked in the past, the student will become the champion of your classroom's attention. How do you expect to beat the champ?

Evel Knievel and Harry Houdini were students at one time. Like many kids, they probably inflicted outspoken grievances to change the daily experience of school to one where mischief could ensue. This chapter is about standing up to bullies. Not the bully who is pestering another child. The bully who is challenging the adult.

Picture yourself in a Western movie in a dusty one-horse town. Ten paces ahead of you stands your opponent with glaring eyes of unbridled defiance. All the eyes of the town are on you, seeing who will falter first. Fists began to grind cautiously in each opponent's palms as each waits for the other to make their move. One sheriff fires the first warning. The outlaw decides a new tactic, nudity.

"Mr. Chippendale, I reckon I told you to not come around these parts no more."

"Sheriff, you know I don't keep my clothes on for no man. I reckon you are going to lose your job today."

"No one wants to see you nude. Put the shirt back on, and we can calmly talk this over with a fruit cup."

The sheriff holds the fruit cup in his hands as a peace offering, but Mr. Chippendale needs the tip money. Now let's go back to the scene of what really happens when Mr. Chippendale decides to follow through with his threat.

When I have three or more students in my resource classroom, I usually have differentiated instruction at each center. Centers are groups of desks placed around the room. Often three or more students will have reviewed a lesson together. Then I will send two or more students to work in a center. The group at this center is in my direct line of sight about fifteen feet away. The independent group will practice skills on their level, and the main idea is for them to work without distracting the students at the teacher-led table. The students at the teacher-led table receive direct instruction and trust the other students working independently will behave civilly. Thus, these centers require an amount of responsibility from the students. This day, this trust is broken.

It seems like any other day. It is late November, and my routines seem to be building a classroom culture. A culture of respect is forming, and at times their improving manners suggest the reversal of the negative reputation earning them the title of culprits. Each student's past behavior is so bad that for the sake of the community, we place these students outside a class of general education students. After gathering the four male students from their respective classrooms, I start a guided reading lesson at my teacher-led table. With heavy shoulders and apathy in his eyes, my soon-to-be-stripper sits down to say, "I am not reading today."

A boy of eight years old decides to object my authority. I issue a warning. Patiently I say, "If that is your choice, then you will not be rewarded with the group game at the end of class."

Going back to the last lesson on group surveys, I tell you that this is the only boy who indicated he did not want a group game as a reward. He wants to act out plays or work on the computer. Since I decided that he would play the group game, what incentive does he really have to behave?

First, he sits at the teacher-led table, staring at the floor while his peers begin reading. He starts to make faces at the other students to get them to laugh. Then I issue another warning. "Start reading your book, or you will have to stay after class to finish your work"

I can see the anger in his eyes. "If you make me read, I am going to take my clothes off," says the would-be Chippendales dancer.

The whole class erupts in laughter. It takes a few minutes to calm everyone down, and now Mr. Chippendales's expression changes from anger to joy. With a smug smile, I send him off to an independent station. He was ruining the lesson for the other students. Chippers had been testing me for weeks with subtle hints that he would take his clothes off. Reflecting on my own teaching steps, I have the hindsight to realize I should have adjusted my reward system to reflect what he indicated on the survey he wanted.

Mr. Chippendales's partner joins him, and their mischievous smiles indicate I have to issue a consequence soon. It takes all but two minutes for these culprits to start playing instead of working. They are trying to discreetly put books in the trash can. I give a stare in their generally direction to show my patience is waning. I hear a whisper: "I dare you. I dare you." The would-be stripper takes my chair with wheels and glides across the classroom.

As I quickly rise, my chair falls over. My inner cowboy comes out.

Stern, I say, "Get to your center, or your recess is gone,"

The child responds, "You take away my recess, and I'm going to take my clothes off!"

All eyes zoom on us as my cowboy stare intensifies. Sweat is forming on my brow as I look at my pint-size opponent. All eyes zoom in on Chippers showing a smile of satisfaction.

Dan, keep your cool, I command myself.

My opponent wants my attention, but more important, he wants me to not enforce the rules.

I move to the board and grab his name. Time moves in slow motion as I turn the safety key to the nuclear device. I begin the teacher's most devastating weapon, the five-second countdown.

"Five."

The room grows silent, and all eyes move in my direction, even the culprit's.

"Four."

The culprit sees eyes on him and, feeling empowered, puts his belt buckle in his hand.

"Three." Crap, I think he is actually going to take his clothes off. I am going to lose my job.

"Two."

I begin to tiptoe toward Chippers, ready to grab him in case he finds a pole and begins disrobing. I see him calculating my intentions and watch him move slowly, inch away from me. I have a dilemma. I am halfway across the room. He can get half his clothes off by the time I reach him. If I don't move his color, he has won. If I do, I might have a naked child. I do not remember reading this scenario in any textbook.

The child cannot win, and this is taking too much time.

"One," I quickly shout. "Your recess is gone. Go ahead get naked; I bet you won't do it."

The class freezes to look at Mr. Chippendale. Within seconds, his shirt is off, and he is down to his underwear, laughing.

I run to grab his arm and scoop up the shirt from the floor. As he flails and kicks, I manage to put the shirt around his neck, but there is no way I can put the shirt around his arms. I realize this is not the best strategy, as my number one concern is that he does not hurt himself. Since I can't manage to put his clothes back on, at least I can restrain the culprit from taking off more clothes.

My remaining students lose their composure. One student decides to get Play-Doh and step on it on my carpet. Noting my total attention to the crisis, another student takes advantage of the situation and throws books on the floor. I now have three of four students in total anarchy.

In desperation, I decide to let go of the culprit and pretend to not care. I focus my attention on the other students and get them back in line by issuing consequences. They apologize and start cleaning up their messes. Meanwhile, Mr. Chippendale, in his Batman boxers, parades around the room searching for more laughs with long struts. I wait for my partially nude student to do one full lap around my classroom until he gets closer to the door. I leap to grab the would-be nudist by the arm and pull him out the door. In the same motion, I lock the door.

"The lock that keeps you inside works both ways," I say with a smile.

The child was not ashamed to get undressed in front of a teacher and students of the same gender. We have big windows by the door in the classroom. My hope is that he will be embarrassed, as this is not acceptable behavior. Thankfully, two girls, age ten, walk down the hall. The look of fear on his face is priceless. By the way, did I mention it is late November, and it is getting really cold?

At a certain age, many young men want to look masculine to women, and Batman boxers usually are not the first choice.

In shock, the student bangs on the class door, begging to return to my classroom. As students pass by laughing and pointing, I think of one last measure to seal my victory. I use my phone to call the front office.

Over the PA system, the voice says, "Principal Laney to room 254. Principal Laney to room 254."

The culprit screams, "Nooooo!" The child darts down the hall, and I release the lock. Just as he turns the corner, he stands right in front of the principal.

The principal's jaw drops, and he grabs Mr. Chippendale by the arm. As he is dragged back to my classroom, I hold up his pants and look at the other students with a stance of triumph.

"Does anyone else want me to tell the girls he wears Batman boxers?"

Their eyes fall to the floor, and I know this cowboy has won…

Teaching Tool 2

Create a Behavior Management System

This scenario did not need to happen. It happened because I lacked the knowledge of how to clearly explain a set of rules and execute consequences. I did not model the rules and consequences to my class. I issued threats and very few real consequences. Issuing threats and not consequences was a big mistake that I am sharing in hopes that it helps others avoid conflict.

I stress that you need four to six weeks to create solid routines and model rules. With guidance from the teacher, the students should help create the rules. This gives students a sense of ownership. When a situation like nudity arises, questions should pop up in each student's mind, such as "Would I want my friends to strip down to their underwear when I am trying to learn?"

Hopefully, they all say no, and the issue is avoided. Additionally, by giving students the chance to give input on the consequence, they feel more responsible for their behavior.

We see this idea in our wider society. Owners usually take better care of property compared with renters. Mostly because they consider the property they buy as an investment. Students need to buy into the classroom culture to minimize crotch grabbing or any other detrimental behavior that distracts from learning.

Creating a behavior management system is necessary to create a safe, challenging, and joyful classroom. These are some tips when creating a behavior management system:

Safety

Safety in the classroom boils down to fairness and security. During the first week of school, I sit students in groups and have them come up with rules. This gives them autonomy and a sense of ownership over their own education. If you want, you can also create a lesson that steers students toward rules that you have selected. This can be done by writing down the rules during a class discussion with student input. Students become emotionally invested and responsible for their actions. Some examples of rules are:

The teacher only acknowledges students who give a nonverbal cue, like three figures showing that they need to go to the bathroom.

Examples of Rules

Take turns the way we agree upon as a class.

Keep your hands and feet to yourself.

Stop what you are doing and put your hands in the air when the bell rings.

Follow the new set of instructions or resume you activities only when the bell rings the second time.

Start each day with a morning meeting. A morning meeting is fifteen minutes at the start of the day when students play a team-building game, and we outline the activities for the day. We may review rules or preview portions of an upcoming lesson that may be challenging. The morning meeting sets the flow for the entire day.

The teacher can create games where each student takes a turn and listens to a classmate's ideas. Modeling how you want the children to act during certain times of the day. Then see if your students can model the same behavior. Model the behavior and have a discussion of how you expect your students to live up to the group's expectations. When the rules are broken, you can refer back to the modeling to reinforce the response the student should have taken instead of breaking the rules. This helps to eliminate excuses students have when a conflict arises.

When students drive the rules and create the consequences, there is a strong sense of fairness. This democratic approach to doling out consequences will keep your own biases out of the situation. The classroom you are creating is one of emotional safety, which tends to have less physical incidents, as students learn to self-regulate their behavior. Inner calm becomes outer calm.

Ideally, each student will pose questions to the other students, giving them the choice to make the right decision.

An example of a good dialogue is:

"Eric, how do we share in a group?"

Ideally, Eric will reply with something to the effect of "We ask first if anyone needs the material, and if everyone says no, I can use it."

This is reenforcing the rules to take turns the same way we as a class agree. If Doug comes to me saying Eric took his materials, I will ask, "Did Eric ask everyone if they were using it?" If Eric and Doug say no, then I can issue a consequence to Eric because he broke the rules.

Again, if you want to have more control, you can create a list of recommendations or reworded student answers that closely match your teacher-made rules. However, I cannot stress enough that these rules should seem like they are coming from the students.

Make Your Lessons Challenging

Even at age five, we want life to have some challenges. How far back can you remember your first major conflict? Every child wants to be a part of a greater story and rise to the occasion. That is why so many of our popular novels revolve around overcoming the odds. When you were a child, did you want more challenges in your day? Maybe you were the lazy one, but did you still get a sense of satisfaction from overcoming an obstacle that was fun?

Giving students more of a choice in their academic day inspires them to take on obstacles. Create a list of norms for your instructional time that they agree to in addition to the rules revolving around safety. If students refuse to participate in your behavior management system, I do not advise taking anything away. Instead, refuse to give them the incentives they want, thus spurring them on to take on challenges for the rewards they seek.

The psychology behind this type of motivation is fascinating. I phrase their rewards in the morning as if they have already earned the incentive. I have noticed if my students feel like they have already earned something, they work harder to keep their privileges. Simply state, "I would really love to give you your earned computer time. I am sorry you did not work hard in your last center to earn it now. However, you have a choice. Go back and finish your work; as soon as you're done jump on the computer."

It's a fair response, and you keep your emotions out of the situation. I could yell, "How could you not complete your work? No computer time for you, buddy. You failed." That's the message when we issue consequences to children and they don't have the opportunity to redeem themselves. We need to give them the opportunity to face and overcome challenges.

Joy

Teachers enjoy incentives, and so do students. Students work hard and need breaks. The younger the student, the more breaks he or she will need. Studies show that high-load tasks that require more attention generally have worse performance than low-load tasks (Betts, J., McKay, J., Maruff, P., & Anderson, V., 2006). High-load tasks can be described as doing fifty math problems compared with low-load, twenty problems. The difference is low-load tasks should involve more thought and steps for how students solve the problem. Students thoughtfully show their work and get less stressed out from not having to complete fifty problems.

To experience joy, we must take the time to take breaks and have physical movement incorporated in the day. Students of any age retain more information when they take breaks and move around. Roy J. Shepard, MD, and François Trudeau, PhD, examined physical activity in correlation to academic performance and found "greater attention and acute gains of mental performance immediately following physical activity."

When to Give a Consequence

Any teacher will tell you to follow through on your threats or students will not respect your authority. There is a balance between issuing consequences and giving the children a chance to redeem themselves. Issuing consequences usually occur when the students are openly defiant. The allocation of consequences should always follow logical steps developed with your students.

Start by issuing a warning to the student to see if he or she can change a behavior. I recommend a warning because this provides a chance for self-regulation. Do this by posing a question to the student so that you can transform a seemingly destructive moment into a learning opportunity. If the behavior was pushing a classmate, you could ask, "Should you be hitting your friend?" or "Would you want someone to hit you?" If he or she continues pushing, that student is defiant, and then you must issue a consequence.

Chippers made threats to take his clothes off for a week and took up precious instructional time. If this showdown happened sooner, maybe the problem would have been corrected sooner. I am not telling you to light the fuse every time you see a spark, but I was just issuing threats, not consequences in prior weeks. I was still allowing Chippers to have rewards even when his behavior was not excellent.

Even when I issued a consequence during my early years of teaching, it was either too harsh or not harsh enough. Worse, my consequences were inconsistent, and the students took advantage of my moods instead of a logical set of rules I laid out. I revamped my rules midyear using these techniques, and those with wild behaviors began to calm down. Here are a few suggestions for logical steps in administering consequences.

Reinforce the positive early, even if you are issuing warnings. Point out students doing the right thing. Give warnings to groups to give everyone the opportunities to correct their actions. After one to two warnings to a group, give a warning to the individuals misbehaving. If the individual does not correct his or her behavior, give the student a consequence. Use a visual behavior system to let students know how they are doing and to indicate when they have not earned an incentive.

Giving individuals a chance to improve their behavior does not atomically mean they get away with breaking the rules. A student who starts a fight needs a phone call home and needs to know he or she will not get a privilege. That student may not have a chance to totally redeem himself or herself that day, but have a system where the student can improve even if the student made a mistake.

After youth break a rule, it becomes critical for you to pose a question to the students. Ask them what decisions they could have made to see if they could generate the right actions. If they don't come up with an adequate response, remind them about previous modeling activities in the classroom or conversations you may have had that are similar to the incident. The younger they are, the more time they might need to process their choice. Set the parameters of how they can improve their behavior. Make it clear. For example, did they keep their hands to themselves, complete four paragraphs in the writing assignment today, or ask friends if they were using the materials? Once they begin to take the suggestions you talked about, reward the students. It might seem like a long cycle of issuing consequences and then giving them a chance to redeem their actions. Well, it is, but most students come around to this fair approach.

What if students continue to be a problem? Issue another consequence and make it more severe. Think aloud for the student, as the seemingly obvious reason to comply to the rules might not seem so obvious for someone who is angry. For example, "John, you realize that if you don't share the game, you will be taking away your own reward of playing on the computer, and now I will have to contact your parents in addition to taking away your computer time. Remember, this will be your choice." When you are talking out loud, students realize you are in tune to their wants.

Notify the parents if none of these strategies work. Maybe there is nothing that can motivate the student at school. However, I am sure that there is something, from a bike to a video game system, that the student loves at home. Have a meeting with the parent(s) to talk about hobbies at home. If parents seem like they do not issue consequences, then you as the teacher need to step up and explain practical steps they can take at home to reward positive behavior.

Not all homes are created equal. What seems like common sense to you may not be for your student's parent. First, suggest a reward for positive behavior at home similar to your classroom's. Suggest getting a timer. Why? Time does not lie. Give a parent a clear consequence system for a certain amount of time. Suggest the parent use the timer for homework. Make sure the parent is issuing a consequence if the student is not following the rules at home. Even invite parents to your classroom to model the same approach for logical consequences at home.

Maybe you are a parent reading this book, and a teacher does not have logical steps in the classroom. Your child is continuing to get in trouble, and the child cannot explain why. If you are a parent, ask the teacher to explain the behavior system in the classroom. If the teacher needs help, recommend this book or another resource.

The lesson I learned from Mr. Chippendale is this student needed to experience a consequence. Not an empty threat but an actionable response to his rebellion. Chippers's computer time and ten minutes from his recess were taken for the rest of the week. He had to write me an apology letter, and video games at his home were taken from his privileges for a month. Because of these consequences, he would have to think twice about threatening to take his clothes off again. Chippers remained clothed for the rest of the year.

Through mistakes we learn to correct our actions. The misunderstanding was that the culprit thought he was the boss. The majority of the time students without clear rewards-and-consequences systems either end up not challenged or test your authority.

Just because you issued a consequence does not mean a student is going to take it gracefully. Look him or her straight in the eye and don't back down. Even if the student tears up your classroom by throwing every book, desk, and chair, issue your consequence. Let the student know the tantrum made it even worse, and keep your cool till the student calms down. Maybe the student has never experienced a consequence. Worse, maybe the student has never been given the chance to redeem himself or herself. In all instances, remember to channel the inner cowboy/cowgirl.

Behavior Management Links

There are hundreds of ideas on how to manage behavior in K–12. If you want a blank template to plan out a behavior plan, use link number one.

1. A great worksheet you can use to plan out your behavioral strategies: http://www.freeprintablebehaviorcharts.com/theme_charts.htm

FBA Link

Your students might need a Functional Behavior Assessment (FBA), a more intense way to record and correct behavior. These are usually completed by social workers or school psychologists. A teacher should ask these professionals if a FBA assessment is the correct choice for your student. By tracking behavior according to antecedent (cause), behavior (action), and consequence (intervention), you can track your strategies in a scientific manner to ward off problems before they start. I find this link really helpful for seeing patterns and getting stakeholders involved in dealing with the problem.

2. FBA scatterplot of your classroom roster to personalize each student's behavior plan: http://www.ped.state.nm.us/RtI/behavior/4.fba.11.28.pdf

Citations

New Mexico Public Education Department Technical Assistance Manual: Addressing Student Behavior, http://www.ped.state.nm.us/RtI/behavior/4.fba.11.28.pdf. Web, Aug 6, 2014.

Betts, J., McKay, J., Maruff, P., & Anderson, V. (2006). The development of sustained attention in children: The effect of age and task load. *Child Neuropsychology, 12*(3), 205–221. doi: 10.1080/09297040500488522

Roy J. Shepard, MD, and François Trudeau, PhD, T., Sallis, J. F., Blizzard, L., Lazarus, R., & Dean, K. (2001). Relation of academic performance to physical activity and fitness in children. Pediatric Exercise Science, *13*, 225 –237.

D isn't a bad word. F... is a bad word

—Kindergartener

3
Monique and One Thousand Pennies!

"Absolutely not," I shout with intensity as I escort Monique from an isolated spot in the cafeteria back to her peers.

The cafeteria has around eighty students eating lunch from grades two to five. Monique has just flung her mac and cheese at Todd for calling her weird. Todd is isolated at a desk after he flung his mac and cheese back at Monique. The floor is dirty with milk, bread crumbs, and noodles. The janitor looks at my class with disgust. I tell Monique and Todd to come back to the group after they clean up their mess. My fuse is running short between these two culprits. When Monique asks to drop off her pennies at the main office I say no. When Monique goes wandering the halls she sometimes returns hours later looking for food.

Monique wants to drop off her thousand pennies to the main office for the penny drive, an annual fundraiser for new playground equipment. I am on lunch duty, and my twenty second graders have to walk across a precarious intersection in the inner city to reach the playground. It would have only taken an extra minute to send the child to drop off the pennies. Maybe I should have sent Monique with a buddy to the principal's office. However, in the school system, minutes add up, and I decline the request.

I am faced with fulfilling the needs of my students and the desire to run an efficient class. These two choices are constantly clashing in which has a higher priority.

The pennies are in a weathered gallon-sized plastic bag. Monique is swinging the bag of pennies as we line up her classmates. The other students are grabbing the bag by the seams. This leads to several small disputes over who has the honor to take the bag of pennies with Monique to the office. The time has come to lead the twenty disciples to the promised land, a land of monkey bars and magical slides. A fond memory all of us have of being free. Stop and think for a minute about your childhood. Do you remember the energy you felt when you heard the word *recess*?

It is time to cross the busy intersection in the inner city. The students are walking out of the stuffy institutional doors and into the bright rays of sunlight. When the sunlight hits their faces, you can see smiles, which is pleasant for me to witness. However, the sunshine does not bring order; it brings primal urges of prancing, kicking, and screaming. This excitement transforms my well-behaved straight line into frolicking children with one student wildly swinging her bag of Abraham Lincolns.

Monique is at the end of the line, and I am focused on another culprit at the front of the line. The students have to walk next to an old wooden retaining wall two feet high. The top of the wall has splinters and is not properly maintained. Monique decides to drag her bag of one thousand pennies along the retaining wall near the end of the intersection.

In an instant, copper fills the sky and rolls across the busy intersection.

"Pennies!"

Just as our ancestors must have yelled in celebration of the discovery of food, my students are transforming into a pack of penny wolves. In a matter of seconds, kids scatter into the intersection, stuffing their dirty pockets full of pennies.

"Get out of the street!" My heart is pounding; their lives are at stake. Tires screech, and I see looks of disgust from pedestrians. One citizen, probably in her eighties, shakes her head and gives me the look only a mom can give. I look for help from the community, but alas, all I see is shaking heads. "Get out of the street now!" My voice becomes hoarse.

There is no response from the penny bandits. Students are being hurled by other students like rag dolls. The heavier culprits use their genetic advantage of superior mass to throw the weaker human specimens against the retaining wall. Pennies are being stuffed in pockets, socks, and God knows where else. I start throwing out consequences.

"Recess is gone for those caught in the street." I start yelling names, and most students run to the sidewalk. I grab the two remaining students as another passing car stops to stare at the mass of small humans crawling on the ground.

I need to gather all the pennies, but I have no bag.

It is early spring, and my thick ski coat has a winter knit cap. "Put all the pennies in my hat or your recess is gone." Exhausted, the wild pack follows my directions. Finally, the traffic resumes, except for Grandma across the street still shaking her head slowly in disapproval.

From all directions, my cap is filled with pennies, and all the students are laughing as the cap starts overflowing with pennies.

After five minutes of chaos, all the pennies are picked up from the street, though several kids still have some in their hands.

Monique is angry. Stomping her feet and pouting, she screams, "Give me back all my pennies!" She screeches as she stretches her hand into a nearby friend's pocket to reclaim her previously scattered currency.

Monique looks at me with pleading eyes. "They still have some of my pennies, and we need the money to get a new playground." As mad as I am at Monique, I cannot let my students steal from their peers.

With reluctance, I moan, "We need to go inside and count all the pennies."

A good old-fashioned shakedown is in order.

Upon entering the building, we pass by the secretary, who stares at us in confusion.

I ask a student to find a trash bag from the janitor. She runs ahead, and we walk with sunken eyes back to the cafeteria.

"Put all the pennies in this bag," I command.

Monique stands with me, now acting as my deputy. "Yeah, put them in this bag," she affirms with a tone of authority.

The children I trust put all the pennies back in the bag. The penny drive is to raise money for the playground; most students understand that if they take these pennies, they will be stealing from themselves. A few culprits do not understand the concept of giving for the greater good. Lucky for me, these second graders have not developed a poker face and are clearly laughing.

Without me asking, Monique is volunteering to reach into snot-filled coat pockets for the playground penny drive. I admire her dedication. Several resist enough that I have to grab their arms to keep them from fleeing. As a teacher, I cannot let these children think stealing from the fundraiser is acceptable behavior. However, the deputy is met with angry faces, as these thieves think they were going to get away with their penny heist.

Finally, Todd responds with a smile indicating he is loving these she-nanigans, "Check my pockets."

The deputy complies, but I notice a wince in his eyes and a shuffle of his feet.

Shakedown time, get against the wall, is what I want to say to the culprit. *Your penny-thieving days are numbered.*

My deputy announces, "I think he has pennies in his shoes."

In a flash, my deputy is on the run after Todd. As the deputy sprints toward the penny bandit, the bandit for some reason starts to skip in an awkward fashion, flailing his arms and screaming in pain from the army of copper assaulting his feet.

At this time, I am guessing the penny thief wishes Monique had gone to Coinstar. My deputy tackles Todd to the floor. I run to separate the two opponents. Monique is violently tearing off Todd's shoes. I look the penny bandit straight in his eyes to enforce the law by saying, "You had your fun—now give the pennies to Monique. Remember, these are for you to have a new playground."

Reluctantly, Todd finds a bench and slouches to remove the pennies. The bandit is not happy he has been caught. His previously white shoes are worn to a shade of a dusty gray, and he takes his time to remove them. As Todd unveils his brownish socks, he takes a deep sigh. To our surprise, some bent baseball cards fall out from deep inside his shoes. His classmates start laughing, and I feel like I want to spew as my deputy scoops her hands into his grimy shoes, double-checking to shake all the pennies loose from his sneakers.

Around twenty pennies spill into Monique's grateful hands.

"Deputy, those pennies are all yours," I say as a slight tingle of bile comes up my throat at the smell of my bandit's feet, and Monique eagerly gathers the remaining pennies from the stained brown socks.

Exhausted, I say, "No recess. This took up all your time."

Everyone looks at Monique with fury.

Monique turns to me and says, "If you had let me take the pennies to the principal's office before recess, none of this would have happened."

"Thanks, Monique. I never would have thought of that." Note to self: teach students about sarcasm.

Teaching Tool 3

Build Routines and Respond to Needs

Have routines to take care of all your students' basic needs and a system to handle special requests. The younger they are, the needier they will be during the day. Additionally, factor movement breaks or brain breaks into your instructional time. A nonverbal system such as three fingers for the bathroom and two fingers to ask a question could be used.

Request Box

For special requests, I have students put four fingers in the air for an immediate response or I motion for them to go to the request box. On a blank slip of paper, the pupils put their questions in a box for later review. The request box is for students who feel they cannot wait. Once they write notes, they feel their needs are met, and the teacher can have fewer interruptions. Set a time for a bathroom break, such as every hour or more, into your session. For high school or middle school, go over the importance of bathroom break in between periods.

Right before lunch and at the end of the day, I review the request box questions and take care of their needs. The box is located right by my classroom's door. This system works when you are in centers or teaching the whole group. Plus, do not be surprised if you get some loving messages. For middle and high school students, you can have students write down their questions in a journal and answer all questions once you are done explaining the lesson.

What if for some reason their needs are not met? For example, they claim they did not go to the bathroom. By following a routine, everyone would use the bathroom during a scheduled time, and everyone should be able to hold it for an hour or two. However, if it does seem like an emergency, I have the students use an *x* symbol with two fingers to tell me it's an emergency.

The idea with a morning meeting, bathroom break, and any other routine is to satisfy their needs. Once their needs are met, your students are in better frames of mind to learn. The request box or any other method you choose is meant to avoid disruptions in your lesson. In hindsight, I should have let Monique drop off her pennies with a buddy. At the time, I did not have a request box.

Acknowledging their wants to avoid interruption is why I created the request box. This makes them feel loved and valued. Asking questions is important for our scholars during a lesson, but many questions are actually a personal request—nothing to do with the lesson.

There are other ways in which you can fulfill students' needs during the day. Answering students' questions as we walk to the bathroom or walking to another part of the building is a great way to address their needs. Questions will allow for the creation of a relationship to form. Questions will need to be posed back to the student to develop higher-order thinking questions. I will address how to use higher-order thinking questions to enhance your lessons in a later chapter.

However, don't let the kids take advantage of you. If they are trying to outsmart you by asking for rewards or unreasonable requests, you still need to say no. The worst-case scenario is that you might have to shake down forty pants pockets full of pennies.

Movement Break

A movement break can support your kinetic learner and satisfy movement needs during a lesson. Get your students' energy out by having interactive lessons in which you move. The movement break can reinforce a skill or just be silly. I have always noticed a huge morale boost around the classroom when the students are allowed to move. The class returns to their desks with the energy and focus to absorb new content. I created a good rule of thumb, to add five minutes for every grade. Starting at kindergarten, have a movement break every twenty minutes. Increase the movement break by five minutes per grade. For a second grader, take a movement break at least every thirty minutes. The older the students' ages, the longer they can sit at their desks. I know the middle grades and above have periods, but giving students a quick movement break during a lesson gets the minds going.

Brain Break

Students who are struggling to think critically after a long lesson may need a brain break. Students burn out when you overwhelm them with hundreds of problems and a tight timeline for students to finish the task in the time you allotted. Focus on analyzing fewer problems and motivate them to work toward a small break. It's amazing that cognitive breaks result in greater academic gains. If you see your students' attention waning, you can trust your gut. Try the same set of questions after a one-to-two-minute break or take a break when you see your students' anxiety increasing.

I hope that you take the time to incorporate routines and breaks in your day to respond to students' needs. We cannot treat youth as robots. We take care of their needs, and the tradeoff is they develop the patience and respect to listen to the mentors in their lives.

I have a headache; it's pissing me off.

—First grader

4

Total Fucking Chaos

When I reflect on my culprits' actions, I see them as little Jedi who do not know how to control their powers. They are experimenting to see which side of the force is stronger. My goal is to have order and support a positive learning environment. Today the students went to the dark side of the force.

Once, a half-used storage closet was my small modified classroom. It had a kidney table with five seats and two large tables with four chairs each at the other end of the room by a door. The room, still used for storage, had books piled in boxes with each stack being five boxes high. I was charged with the task to teach the students specific skills in a small-group environment. It began when I did not give Spider Man a break, and out of anger he found a window ledge to climb onto.

"Get off that window!" I shout as Spider Man climbs onto the tiny strip of wood by the window. Seeing that my attention is drawn to our resident superhero, Mark decides to grab a marker and draw on the whiteboard, destroying the lesson I had in place.

As I hold a flailing Spider Man, I grab for the marker in Mark's hand. This immediate reaction causes my once-firm grip to falter, and Spider Man makes a superhero jump from the precarious edge.

With horror, I watched him jump three or more feet, thus catapulting his limber body by the stack of poorly arranged boxes. Spider Man lands triumphantly on the carpet and says, "That was fun. I want to do it again."

Mark grabs another marker to continue to draw on the whiteboard. At first it looks like a normal family portrait, but once completed, one character has an unusually large rear end.

I grab Mark just as Spider Man completes another spinning jump, this time with the completion of a Chuck Norris–approved roundhouse kick. As he grazes the stack of books, they wobble for a slow ten seconds. I fear they will topple on our hero. How would I explain to his parents that the knowledge we sought to teach him for good became the villain that crushed him? What a plot twist.

I am able to grab Spider Man on his second landing. Holding a child in either arm is a challenge. However, I have three other students present in the classroom. They are laughing uncontrollably at Spider Man aerobics and Mark's mural until Mark yells at Gwen, "Hey, Gwen, I drew your mom's big butt!"

It is on like Donkey Kong. Mark should have recalled the last person who embarrassed Gwen. Gwen is the same physical size as Mark, but her spirit is mightier. Gwen has masculine shoulders, is a forward for the soccer team, and is unusually tall for her age. Gwen's laughter ceases as she violently flips a desk. In shock, I let go of Mark.

I watch a history lesson unfold. We will call Gwen Germany and Mark Poland.

Blitzkrieg!

Germany pummels her fists in a circle motion like a cartoon, while Poland is absolutely stunned. I try to protect Poland from the on-slaught of Germany with behavior sanctions. These sanctions are my consequences, but they have no effect.

"No recess for either of you if you don't stop."

The fists continue to spin.

"I am calling you parents."

The once-brave insult-thrusting Mark is now reduced to a small ball moaning in the fetal position.

"I am calling Principal Laney!" I issue the Hail Mary of all threats.

"Don't make fun of my momma," Gwen yells as sweat begins to form on her forehead.

Spider Man is screaming at Gwen, "Leave my friend alone!"

Mark is now in tears, pleading, "I'm sorry my mom has a big butt too; don't hit me; please stop!"

The reader might be thinking, *Why does the teacher not get between Gwen and Mark to stop the fight?* Remember, it is a blitzkrieg, and I am being rapidly attacked on two fronts. If I let Spider Man go, I will have an all-out brawl. Plus, Mark is learning a valuable lesson in humility.

I remember my Jedi training to use positive incentives, as my threats to take away privileges have no effect on my students.

My two other students sit patiently at their desks, staying neutral. Let's call them Switzerland. "Stop! Everyone, look at Switzerland," I exclaim with a smile. *Look at all their years of economic prosperity.* I mean, "Look how my two friends at the table are not fighting. They are sitting at their desks, and I don't have to hold them down," I say sarcastically, which thankfully these students have not developed the ability to detect.

"Wow, I think Switzerland deserves to play one of our favorite games on the computer," I say with a big smile.

Gwen stops hitting Mark, as computer games are her favorite incentives, as indicated by her survey.

Gwen walks calmly and sits back at her desk.

With swollen, tear-filled eyes, Mark looks at me as if to ask, is the war over?

My attention shifts to Mark. "You are going to erase the drawing on the board and apologize to Gwen, because I have seen better behavior than this. I know you can work hard to earn back your computer time as well."

Wiping the tears from his face, Mark walks toward the board, clearly defeated. He slowly erases the board while Gwen intently looks for an apology.

Mark sheepishly responds, "I'm sorry."

The positive reinforcement is starting to work, and I say, "Great, you are sitting up straight and you seem ready to learn. Get out your math journal for problem of the day; we need to earn that computer time back." Four students pull out their journals and begin working.

I am still holding a wiggling Spider Man, who signals he is not convinced computer time is the positive incentive for which he strives.

"What's wrong, Spider Man?" I moan.

"I want to keep jumping from the window. I want to be super," he begs.

I take a moment to comprehend his words. Partly for my sanity and partly to develop a relationship with this child. Realizing he wants positive praise for his jumping, I muster up what energy I have left to exclaim, "Those were excellent jumps, especially the one with the kick. Where did you learn those moves?"

"Spider Man and Ninja Turtles movies," he replies as if I might not have ever heard of these superheroes before. It is almost as if he is trying to show me his value he is bringing to the classroom. Yes, the initial teacher response is to reprimand, but I need to acknowledge and praise his actions.

"How about you show me those moves at P.E. when you have a mat? That way you can really show me your jumping ability."

He agrees and goes to his seat.

"I need to tell you something. My mom has a big butt too. One time I even jumped off it."

"Spider Man, I believe you."

Teaching Tool 4

Positive Reinforcement

How did this chaos start? First, I refused to give Spider Man a break as he began spinning on the carpet. We start each day with math drills on the rug. My speed was slower than normal, running us well past the typical time of our routine. I should have given Spider Man a break. The result was the inability for Spider Man to remain still.

Second, I told Spider Man, "Because you are spinning, we are going to keep going until you participate." I should have had the scheduled break and continued the activity after the break. Spider Man took to releasing his energy and ruining the lesson for everyone. What I thought would work would be to issue consequences. I focused on the negative, and it just made the situation worse. What I should've done was reinforce the positive actions I saw in the classroom earlier in in the day. Sometimes consequences work, and sometimes positive praise works; unless you ask the students directly how they want to be reminded to stay on task, you will need to experiment.

Spider Man's intention was not to be unruly but for me to acknowledge the positive actions he was displaying in protecting the classroom as our superhero. He has pent-up energy not released during the scheduled break. This in turn broke our contract, and he had less incentive to follow the rules. Beyond his physical requirements, what he emotionally needed was what we all need, to be validated. Since Spider Man's needs were not met from an exercise break, and since I did not give him the emotional validation he needed, I had anarchy. This simple strategy, called positive reinforcement, is what I often use first before issuing a consequence.

By simply highlighting the positive behavior of two students behaving correctly, I used my innocent students to turn the tide of a seemingly uncontrollable situation. Some teachers I have encountered do not advocate positive reinforcement. This is from a more militant stance on teaching. Every word out of a teacher's mouth is followed, but the problem is there is no buy-in to this system. Students respond out of fear, but as soon as they are released from the environment, they return to their rebellious nature. In times of great need, when taking away privileges and the fear you instilled has failed, you must use different resources from your toolbox.

My classroom culture has made a huge shift from having negative consequences to having positive reinforcement strategies I administer daily. I am constantly giving words of affirmation, giving high fives, and displaying student work. Act the way you want to feel is my motto. Even though some days I force the enthusiasm, I can say that my children look forward to the positive aura I deliver. Children seek your approval in any fashion. It is your choice whether you want to respond to your children by being negative or positive. Their actions will take many forms to get your attention. However, what you dish out is often what you will get in return.

Here are eight positive examples you can get their attention and correct behavior:

- Positive group redirection: I like what [name] is doing. Everyone look at [name].

- Individual positive redirection: Can you work like [name]? Good job that deserves a high five.

- Positive group redirection: I am going to pick the best work sample, and that student will read his or her work out loud.

- Individual positive redirection: Is that a good choice? Could you tell me a better way to act?

- Positive group redirection and showing individual work on the outside of the classroom for other peers to see: A 5/5 goes on the "smart cookie wall."

- Positive reward for groups or individuals: Three students will be chosen to spend some time with the teacher at lunch or in a small group doing a fun activity for the best work I see.

- Positive incentive using a gift: Whoever does [desired action] gets [this reward]. (Go back to your survey. Some students may like gifts as the reward. One trick is to have students pick out their gifts and have them visible during the day as a reminder for them to stay on task.)

- Positive group redirection: Jack is doing a great job. Can anyone do it better?

Ultimately the choice to set the positive tone for your classroom is up to you.

Links

https://www.pbis.org A great link to use that shows the advantage of positive intervention strategies

When I grow a beard, can I keep a nest with birds in it?

—Third grader

5
Spiderman

With one knee and a firm hand pressed tightly to the floor, a stoic face rises high in the fluorescent light. It can only be Spider Man!

Eyes blazing, he looks intently in my direction for the acknowledgement of his services.

I give him the approval he is seeking. "Spider Man, can you help me save the day?"

We are on a mission, and that mission is to add to twenty.

As a team, we have three clues to help us reach our unknown answer. The steps on the whiteboard read, *Circle, Find, Leap*. Those steps are the only ones we have to save the day. However, Spider Man can only celebrate a victory if the citizens gave him a wink. Would he be able to find the answer?

I let Spider Man circle the bigger number on his page. With a stare of pure intensity, he says, "I have the power." On the floor, the numbers range from zero to twenty. He must circle the bigger number and leap from the number line on the floor. Spider Man finds his number, seven.

"Please, Spider Man, we need you to find the answer, or all hope will be lost," I say. Then Spider Man has to leap onto the other number to solve the equation. For example, if he circled seven, he starts at seven on the number line. The other number is four. Spiderman leaps four times, and now understands seven plus four equals eleven.

When he arrives at the right answer, a wink is given. The smile that comes across his face is of intense joy. For weeks, I was trying to tame Spider Man to be like every other student. Sit still, sit up straight and do what you're told. He did not comply. There was too much energy and not enough adventure. Once I finally decide to give him the incentive he wants, the distracting behavior in the classroom stops. Spider Man sits for the lesson as long as I give him a break and make the lesson an adventure.

"Did I save the day?" he asks.

"Yes, you did, Spider Man," I say. "Please do ten more problems on paper, and then you can jump again on the floor."

Every teacher needs data, and Spider Man had refused to write on paper. Unless it was a depiction of the battles his imagination wages, he was bored. He is in special education because we had come to a point where his refusal to do work pushed him back behind grade level. He would do flips instead of write or hop instead of read. He is his own source of entertainment.

The interesting conclusion to the Spider Man story is that he eventually began following the rules of his regular classroom. Spider Man is so excited to leap to save the day he will do just about anything we ask to come into the classroom to leap on the floor. We use this advantage to get him to start writing. We finally are able to gather data on his progress. We are able to improve his academics and start to tame his imagination to a specific time of the day. Do not worry—we do not hinder his creativity. We just make it so that Spider Man can function in society.

Teaching Tool 5

Tracking Data

Spider Man is one of my favorite students. With a height of three feet and a tall torso for his age, he is built to be an athlete, an energetic ball of freedom. He has no intention of backing down from his beliefs. We did not always communicate well, as seen by the previous chapter. Spider Man is constantly lost in a world of imagination. It constantly looks like he has a great time battling villains in his head. He wants abundant adventures: battles, space aliens, and his heroics to save the day. The problem was he did not care to produce work at school. That is a problem if you are a teacher who needs more data on a report card than comments on jumping ability.

I decided after the fucking chaos incident I would get work completed if I honored his survey response. Spider Man wants positive reenforcement, and our olive branch was to reward what was right before our eyes. I had him dress up in a Spider Man mask and go out to classrooms, giving out tokens. This is our schoolwide incentive program to reward good behavior. He loves to be a superhero. I would literally pick him up and carry him into classrooms; he was over the moon with joy. The next week I would take away the Spider Man mask unless his behavior was exceptional; it was not exceptional. For two weeks he fought coming to the group or participating in class.

I asked him, "What would a superhero do, give up or persevere?"

One day I put the Super Man mask on the board with a magnet. It was in clear view the entire lesson. When I saw his attention waning, I asked him, "Would a hero give up or persevere to defeat his homework?"

He signed and mumbled, "Persevere."

Spider Man realized we have the power to validate his heroics. He began to join the classroom discussions. We started to see immediate growth. Finally, we were able to control his actions, and he was motivated to learn in order to be able to fly into classrooms. Thankfully, there was no more jumping off window ledges. I was able to get work samples to gather the data I needed. I progressively changed the policy that he had to work hard and follow the requirements we had agreed on four out of five days to be Spider Man Friday afternoon.

I fondly remember those superhero days. I remember the look on his face when he would dress up. I remember the joy and anticipation of him descending into a classroom to reward others. He would scream, "You're unbelievable!" at the top of his lungs to commend his fellow heroes for amazing behavior. Recalling the parent-teacher conference, the tears in his mother's eyes justified the changes we saw in our resident superhero.

My goal was not to break his creative spirit. In fact, I hope I nurtured his morals. Spider Man wants his work to be fun, he wants to have a purpose, and he wants adventure. Why should I extinguish his purpose? Why not shift his purpose toward helping others?

When I reflect on what that Spider Man taught me, it was to never let go of your dreams. Spider Man taught me how to live without fear. A fearless, empowered six-year-old totally rooted in his identity. We did not break his identify—we taught him how to use his powers for good. The school could join the story or go home. Occasionally when I feel down and out, I think about Spider Man. His persistence and warm heart put my faith back in mankind. I encourage my readers to stand up for your identities and beliefs. Be a hero or dance like no one is watching. Spiderman Fridays: they are awesome!

An Overview of Tracking Your Data

Data, data, data. That word will haunt you over and over again as a new teacher. It is important to have data, but it needs to be meaningful data. My advice for you is to have two types of data sheets. First, find the formal ones that match up with your curriculum. Hopefully, you will be teaching with a program that has unit assessments with skills around your lessons. Use those data tracking sheets especially if you are having trouble with your lesson plans.

Next, find a blank template online for tracking your data, by googling *teacher data trackers*, or something to that effect. Keep your student work samples in one binder per skill. By skill, I mean, if your unit is around fractions with remainders, keep results from that test in a separate binder. I find it helpful in managing the disorganization that comes with multiple work samples.

Then, plan to have your lessons in a unit last four to six weeks. Review who will need response to intervention (RTI) extra support in the coming unit. I have also used Excel to plug in the information, which cuts down on the papers lying around your classroom. The key is organization, and having all test results in one binder or Excel spreadsheet will save you time and energy.

Last, give students a preassessment at the beginning of the unit and then a final exam after four to six weeks. Use your end-of-unit test results to drive the direction of your lessons. This system will help you create the lessons your pupils need to be successful. My suggestion is to administer a test or exit slip every Friday to adjust your lesson plans for the end of unit exam.

To sum it up:

- Create data sheets that track standard curriculum or the standard you are working on measuring four to six weeks of progress.

- Give students a preassessment at the beginning of the unit and an exit slip every Friday to adjust your lessons for the final exam.

- Use your final exam to determine which students need RTI and determine which standards to cover in your next unit.

How do I use this data to build my next unit?

Whether you like it or not, in the United States the Common Core Standards are being adopted in many states. These standards are built to be sequential. I recommend writing a standard down on a blank data tracking sheet or in your unit plans. If the majority of students master your unit, find the next sequential skill in your grade level and use that standard for your next unit. The Common Core Standards have already given you a rough guideline of what to teach next.

Tracking your data is necessary for differentiating instruction and challenging your students. A student who has not shown growth per your final exams, even if he or she is above grade level, indicates he or she needs different work. All students should be challenged. When you see poor tests results, don't give up—reflect on what you can do differently. There might be another voice in your head asking, *What are these units being measured by?* Which leads me to the next useful piece of data collection, a rubric.

What are these units being measure by?

A rubric, either teacher made or provided by your administration, should be used to calculate students' results. A rubric is a helpful tool to view the logical steps students are missing in their work samples. For example, let's look at a math word problem. Are they able to support their answers using drawings with a supporting equation? Can they justify their arguments in paragraphs on how they solved the problem with a counterexample? Can they show their steps in how they solved the equation? Maybe a student can answer two out of three of these questions in a word problem. However, students may vary in their answers, and that is why I prefer to use a rubric with a grid that measures each teaching point I am evaluating.

The rubric should be measurable and obtainable. List a percentage to gain mastery. As your experience in teaching grows, you will be able to make your own rubric to challenge every student. Another popular term you will hear is Response to Intervention, meaning students below grade level will need to have an intervention program to boost their grades. There are hundreds of RTI programs across the country. Ask your administrator what programs that school has in place to help struggling students.

This resource is an RTI tracking link for your reference.

Links

http://www.rtinetwork.org/checklists

I'm tired. I think my batteries have died.

—Second grader

6

I Got Baptized, and I Saw the Devil

What is normal? I think when a set of actions or ideals is seen as routine, it is labeled normal.

Daniel is an introvert with the ability to make off-the-wall comments. Shifty eyes and the slow movement of tapping fingers foreshadow his diabolical plots. We try our best not to ask him open-ended questions. Daniel would ramble on with his stories of mischief over the weekend. The teachers and his classmates would shake their heads in unison for his stories were inappropriate for the classroom. It is a Monday; hyper children indicate they are not ready to sit still. Daniel walks in slower than the rest with a smug look on his face. An instructional aid and I call Daniel to my desk.

"Daniel, what did you do this weekend?" I ask with some hesitation.

"I think I strangled a cat."

With that statement, I realize that the luxury of my sheltered weekend is over, and I am back to dealing with little crazy people.

I proceed to ask, "Did the cat die?"

"No, I just watched it try to breathe."

Well, isn't that special. I ponder being rendered speechless.

Trying to compose myself after the shock of this statement and the realization that I am educating the next Hannibal, I think of other children disturbed at the age of nine. When they go crazy, I wonder if there is a selection process in their minds. Do they ask themselves, *Should I hurt or harm this person?*

I decide that this is a great time to whip out the emergency cookies to test my theory.

"Daniel, I am so sorry about that cat. I hope it was OK. Remember, we are your friends, and friends should eat cookies together. Today happens to be cookie day; your friend wants to give you a cookie. I have an idea. Every time you don't strangle living things, let's eat a cookie together. How do you like that as a plan?"

"Well, I do like cookies…" Weighing the options in his mind takes a lot longer than I had hoped.

He starts eating the cookie, and another half-crazed Hannibal smile emerges.

"OK, deal. I also went to church this week."

"Great!" I exclaim. *Please, God, this boy needs Jesus.* My hope for him becoming a functional human being to restore.

"The only thing was they baptized me, and everyone was saying, 'Praise Jesus,' and talking about angels," he says, tapping the table one finger at a time.

"What did you see?" I inquire.

"Well, when I got baptized, I saw the devil."

My joyful face changes to an expression of shock. I do not know what to say, and we need to start the instructional day.

Out of self-preservation, I say, "Later on in life, remember who used to give you cookies."

Teaching Tool 6

Creating Centers or Stations

Situations like these really happen, and you have to think on your feet. Most of my stories follow a template of how things went awry and a correlating lesson. This one does not follow that format. Daniel has the full support of the school system, from a psychologist to a mentor program. The animals are safe. However, for two years, the stories that came out of Daniel I cannot even put in print. This teaching tool is about how to create a gift for all teachers, the center or station.

The center or station idea was created so teachers can have more individual time with each student and develop responsibility in students working in groups with loose parental supervision. Essentially, by creating centers, you are giving yourself the chance to discover learning gaps to better teach each individual student. Plus, you are giving students the chance to complete working independently and practice life skills every person needs.

Centers usually are a physical location in your room: a group of desks or an area with a predefined activity. One physical area may be the fluency workshop. Each group rotates to a center according to ability at a predefined time.

CENTERS AND STATIONS

DIRECT INSTRUCTION

READING COMPREHENSION

20 MINUTE ROTATION

WRITERS WORKSHOP

FLUENCY

Why should I have centers and stations?

What is self-sufficiency? The dictionary defines it as survival. One goal I as an educator see being neglected in your school system is the social emotional piece. Schools need to prepare minors and even culprits for the real world. As the academic years progress, so does the need for students to do more work better in groups. Flash-forward thirty years, and your student is working a job with four team members. The boss assigns a task to the group, to solve a problem. The team must write a proposal showing the most efficient way to distribute the company's products to ten stores. Jim, your former student, never really played well in centers at school. Jim did not share responsibilities and would take credit for work he did not produce. Jim might not have a job for much longer.

Centers, or some may call them stations, build skills for youth to be able to function with a team. In accordance with this idea, school systems are now pushing the use of centers. You can still teach students in a whole-group setting, but when you put in the work to create great centers, the dividends are huge.

Difficulties in managing centers

Giving minors the freedom to work at centers means you have to deal with students finishing early, give appropriate work at centers, and managing behavior. These pitfalls keep many teachers from facilitating centers in their classroom. However, once you have built a system where everyone student is actively learning, and you have five hands raised at your teacher-led table as opposed to twenty hands raised in a whole group, you can better manage the learning of each student.

Students finishing early

Checklists are a magnificent way for students who finish early to keep busy. How many times has a parent or teacher been told by a child, "I'm done"? On the checklist, have students complete the same activity but with a different book. "OK, you're done with that activity; now compare and contrast the characters in both books you are reading." Suggest a scavenger hunt on the checklist or have a requirement for how much work needs to be complete. Can they play a game at the center? Can they play the game again until the time comes you have to rotate to a new center? The answer to all these questions should be yes. The key is to have your groups staying active with each center while you can instruct a group of four to six pupils at your teacher-led table without interruptions.

Appropriate work at centers

Having appropriate work at each center can be a time-consuming challenge. Here are some tips to make sure activities flow smoothly for each group who visits the center.

Model, model, model. I cannot emphasize this point enough. I have even taken a whole day at the beginning of the month to model each activity at each center.

Modeling your center activities is a great way to check for student understanding of the activity and to address potential problems that you discover when you see students trying the activity for the first time. As a bonus, playing a game gives the teacher a break from direct instruction, and everyone has fun modeling the game together. There are two ways to model an activity before releasing a group to a center or station.

Teaching each center by whole group is one method. We can go over to each station one at a time and check for understanding. Four to six students work at the center while the other students watch. The main problem I have with this scenario is that when I was an inclusion teacher, we had to further differentiate the stations. Each group was a color, and when the students went to that station, they had to work on the material that was their group's color. This allows for everyone to be challenged and busy.

Once the initial six weeks of school are over and your centers are flowing, you could slowly introduce a new center at the teacher-led table. The whole reason you have groups is to split students according to academic level. Since the groups are split and coming to your table, you can teach each group's activity at the teacher-led table. Ideally, this system allows for personalized feedback to each student in a smaller group.

The next steps in creating appropriate work at stations is creating the category of work at each station. Usually there are stations for math and literacy. Literacy includes work in fluency, writing, and vocabulary. For math, one station could be working with math manipulatives. For example, blocks that show units in base tens teach a student to add by tens and see the physical representation of the unit of ten. The child adds by using tens blocks (manipulatives), and now you have a kinetic tactile center activity for the student who has been struggling to add.

All students need a brain break. It is important for students to have a lighter cognitive load during center time. Centers should be equal parts joy and work. It also gives the students something to look forward to during centers. Finally, it keeps your students occupied, allowing you to properly do your job.

Just as we adults work for money, so students want to work for a reward. I use some stations for incentives during the school day. They could be educational computer games or board games that incorporate learning. If a student is misbehaving, he or she is prohibited from participating in the fun center.

Here is a list of ideas you can use to give appropriate work at centers.

- Level the complexity of work at each center. If work in Folder B is harder than work in Folder A, teach students to do work in Folder A, if the task is too challenging.

- Have a premade quiz students can take if they feel like they want to move to the next level. If a student passes, allow him or her to work in Folder B, which is harder material. Another option is to assign who will work with each folder before they get to the center. There is no limit to the amount of folders you can make to accommodate every student.

- A short quiz or exit slip each Friday to check for understanding from each group. Gather the data and modify the center.

Managing behavior

Managing behavior at each center can be a challenge for we all know there are students who don't get along with their peers. If you do not trust certain students, what can you do? Plus, how will these groups move about the classroom? These are some tips I use when orchestrating my rotation of centers.

In the first four to six weeks of school, practice rotating from center to center with a timer. Set high expectations, and have students repeat the rotation to each center until they transition in the time frame you allow. If you want all students to move from Center One to Center Two by ten seconds on a timer, then have the class practice until they can make it to each center in ten seconds.

Beyond teaching the whole group to flow efficiently to each center, here is a list to managing individual behavior.

- Pair your problem child with a student who can keep that child accountable to finish work and be agreeable.

- Even with a group of four at a center, require that students still work in pairs.

- Have a positive behavior-intervention checklist at each desk for students with behavioral concerns. This should be a reward system when you see the student is behaving to your expectations. My advice would be to only have reward systems where you give rewards and not to take away privileges.

- To go one step further, give your students with behavior issues a dry-erase board or clipboard. This is to use as a visual reminder. Have the child check off what he or she has accomplished academically or behaviorally. "Did I complete my assignment? Did I keep my hands to myself? Did I help a friend?" Students can check off the list feeling accomplished.

- Have a fix-it chair where students can take a break to amend their actions.

- Have visual cues and reminders at each center.

- Do not forget the nonverbal cues in an effort to avoid interruptions. For example, two fingers can mean "Can I get a tissue?" Look at the student and point at the tissue box. Nonverbal language is used, and it will hardly interrupt the small group you are teaching.

Technology

Why not use technology as a center? An ever-increasing wave of testing and research shows the tailored advantages of online education. Studies support that learning by using technology can significantly increase academic gains. Technology is an integral part of our modern society. A report by National Research Council states that computer games "motivate learners with challenges, rapid feedback and tailor instruction to individual learners' needs and interests" (National Research Council). Get rid of the word *game*, and society finds the research more credible. Teachers and parents must realize technology even when a game is involved can target a skill a student desperately needs to learn.

To sum it up

Centers are useful for managing the classroom and will challenge a pupil within a group at a similar academic level. With good extension activities, the possibilities for a student to practice needed skills and the time spent for the teacher to lead a small group should be endless. This sacred time were students should remain busy when you are teaching a small group is priceless. Centers give you a chance to dig deep and help struggling students at the teacher-led center. The gift of a center is the ability to teach a small group without distractions.

Citation

National Research Council, Margaret A. Honey and Margaret L. Hilton, Editors Science Through Computer Games and Simulations, Washington, DC, 2011.

This is a circle, this is a square, this is a rectal.

-Kindergartener

7

Birth of the Ooze

Marques is a well-lubricated machine of drool, constantly biting his fingernails, pencils, or innocent bystanders. The child can't keep his hands to himself, while everyone desperately wants him to. This kid has fluid coming out of his ears!

Marques is very intelligent. I have to create lessons that are challenging enough for him to gain his attention. His behavior and lack of discipline are what originally placed him in special education. Marques will either dunk his mouth retainer in a girl's milk or sneeze in your general direction to gain attention. One part nerd, one part rebel, one big headache.

Today we are writing an opinion piece. The class is comparing two similar topics from two different authors. The general education teacher and I have split the classroom into four groups. Marques is not with my group, but from a distance I see him stick out his tongue, indicating he wants to lick a female. A boy of eleven years old, he is becoming aware of his fondness for the opposite sex. Later in the year, we will have the birds and the bees talk. I have not had time to discuss that licking is usually an unacceptable courting practice. The girl scurries away from Marques while he has a big smile on his mischievous face.

I am teaching an inclusion small group of four students at a small kidney bean–shaped table. Inclusion means I am helping teach the standard curriculum the students are working on inside the general education classroom. I have several students to teach that day, including Marques. Marques's group works nearby as I teach my group. Marques is trying to stay on green, which is his behavior monitoring tool. Different colors indicate how he is doing at any given moment. At any given moment, it is most likely Marques is not on green. He is chewing on a pen, and pens are not allowed in class. What color is he on again? My thoughts wander as I view his bright-red tongue gnawing on the plastic end of the pen. I regain my attention and look at his behavior chart, not surprised Marques has not obtained the coveted green status.

I see my special friend out of the corner of my eye, cracking jokes and picking his nose. The girls scoot farther away in disgust. Marques takes this as a no-means-yes scenario. *They are rejecting me. I guess that means they want more boogers,* he thinks. Now I understand that when I go to a bar and see that guy in the corner, he is the nose picker twenty years in the future.

I see him chewing on his contraband pen with a smirk on his face. Too busy with my group to warrant another reprimand, I ignore the obvious fact an illegal pen is in the classroom. I hear a snap; the pen cracks, oozing black ink all over his mouth and light-yellow polo shirt. He groans in pain. I am sure the ink does not taste like candy. He makes a hacking noise and the whole classroom shouts, "Ewww!!!"

A student adds, "Spit it out!"

I quickly rise out of my chair to assess the commotion. As Marques turns his head, he spits black ink all over my shirt and forever traumatizes two eleven-year-old girls with the remains of a Bic pen. There was always that one kid in school, that kid with allergies constantly hacking up something vile; yes, that kid is reincarnated as Marques. Yellow mucous and the black pen paralysis our psyche. We stand motionless. *Think happy thoughts,* I try to lie to myself, but reality is sinking in.

Poison control does not have an official classification for this flesh-eating disease that is Marques's spit mixed with black ink, but the combination is something the Center for Disease Control fears might become airborne along the lines of Ebola. I share a look of disgust with the two girls at the desk as we all look at our clothes. We have just spent the past fifteen seconds—at least—exposed to a toxin for which no antibody exists.

Clearly, the token will be revoked.

I look at my shirt and then at Marques without saying a word. Marques looks down at the ground with shame, clearly aware that his token is toast.

It was an accident, and moving him on red would be the worst consequence. Yellow is the color his name will dwell on today. Marques is always on the cusp of moving to green, but blowing it exceptionally. Earning the color red is a deliberate act of defiance, like hitting another student. Marques is more of a taunter. I keep him on yellow because I need hope; he could change. Plus, we need to keep the host alive to create an antibody. With all my strength, I encourage him to apologize to the girls and give him another opportunity to work toward green.

He says, "I'm so sorry." He seems sincere.

The girls and I go to clean off our clothes and try our best to resume the lesson. Each student presents an opinion piece to the class. Marques tries to redeem himself and does an adequate job of presenting his opinion. He compares and contrasts both articles, and the licking gestures cease. As the students line up to go to music class, I call Marques over for a private conference.

"Marques, you made one big mistake today. Do you understand why we do not use pens in the classroom?" He nods. "Since you had a rough day, I am going to give you a prize anyway."

For Marques, his love language is gifts. His token will be redeemed at the end of the day for a small toy. I walk to my pirate-inspired toy chest bought at the dollar store and look through the chest to find a specific toy. His perplexed eyes track my movements.

He appears dazed. I have yet to show him this type of compassion. I pull out a long, straight woven device, and he looks at me, confused. "What is it?" he asks.

"It's a Chinese finger trap. Let me show you." I slip it on his fingers

"Hey, I am trapped! I can't get my fingers out! How am I supposed to get anything done today?"

Exactly. It's a metaphor for our relationship," I say, grinning.

"What is a metaphor?" he asks.

"Hopefully, by the time you figure it out, we will no longer have exploding pens."

Teaching Tool 7

Differentiate Your Instruction

Beyond the funny tale of a gross kid exploding pens in his mouth, you as the teacher will have to create multiple lessons on the same topic for your class. *Differentiating instruction* is the common term you will hear for this strategy. A simple definition of *differentiating* is "to modify the lesson to make the content accessible to all students."

Differentiating has two forms: differentiating the lesson to the whole class, which involves using different modalities to reach a wide array of learners and differentiating to a target group of students who need specific strategies and who learn best by other modes. The broad learning styles can be described as kinetic, auditory, and visual. My goal is to try and incorporate as many learning styles into a lesson as possible and have supports in place to help struggling learners.

Once you incorporate kinetic, auditory, and visual learning styles, then you can differentiate by what I call learning modes. Students could learn pictorially. Meaning, they draw the math equation using pictures to make representations of the numbers. Another mode could be an abstract method of solving math problems with math manipulatives. Blocks could represent values to be added. Again, the goal is to model the same lesson but create a different mode for all learners to access the content.

Let's say the area of concern is multiplication. We have been using repeated addition as a strategy. Repeated addition is like saying five times four is the same as five plus five plus five plus five. The class will count five, ten, fifteen, twenty and stop because they have counted each group of five four times. One group could do this in their heads because they are auditory learners. The other set of students could group an array of objects pictorially as their mode to understand the equation.

A student struggling with numerical comprehension might need multiple modes or strategies to grasp a concept. Again, I call them modes, as opposed to learning styles, as I feel the term *learning style* is too broad. Hence, the teacher should allow students to experiment with different modes to solve five times four, as they all reinforce the same skill. Teachers should not assume how a student will learn best. Allowing for multiple modalities is important for students to discover what methods work best for them. They may only be struggling because the material needs to be presented in a different way.

Ways to make your lesson different?

There are multiple ways in which you can make a lesson different. When you list your steps on the whiteboard, did you write the steps only as verbal steps for the auditory learners? Imagine I write on the whiteboard:

1.) Put a star by the main idea of the article.

2.) Underline the supporting details.

3.) Write a one-paragraph summary of your information.

If I were to write those steps on the board and add nothing else to these written words, what modalities did I miss? I ask myself how I can reach multiple modalities, and is there an example present for the students to follow?

I stop to reflect and then redesign my lesson showing an example of the end product. I think, *These steps seem like an auditory list of actions the students need to use. To incorporate different learning styles and modalities, I would take a short story and model how I want the students to follow these steps.* Now that I have my idea, I can add on to my first step. I start by having a sample article on the board. I visually put a star by the main idea by the example paragraph on the whiteboard, next to my step. Then, with the same article in front of the student, he or she will kinetically put a star by the main idea. The teacher is addressing learning styles, which is the basic overarching theme to make the lesson accessible to more students.

Improved Sample Lesson

1.) Put a star by the main idea in the article. 2.) Underline the supporting details. 3.) Write a one-paragraph summary of your information.	*Jim loves to study the history of the American Civil War. Jim recently went on a trip to Gettysburg with his family to <u>be a character in a Civil War reenactment</u>. After he returned from the trip, <u>he wrote an essay</u> about his experiences and what he learned on his family vacation. Jim hopes to one day <u>study history in college</u>.

The lesson above might seem obvious that with an example the lesson will be better. However, you would be surprised by how simply some teachers present their material with no examples. Many new teachers do not model or work through a sample problem before releasing the student to produce similar material. Without examples and multiple modes being addressed, you are doing a disservice to your pupils.

Once the teacher incorporates multiple modalities, then the teacher can use scaffolding. *Scaffolding* is a term for extra academic support. The educator can target specific learning interventions for each struggling student by having premade materials that will help the student understand the content. The scaffolding is the push and support for the pupil to understand the material at the same academic level as their peers.

A scaffolding technique is to model the steps and give a problem-solving checklist, putting more support in place to carry the cognitive load when the student is going through the steps on the checklist. Eventually, when the student gets the concept, the scaffolding goes away, and the pupil in on grade level.

Here are some more differentiating strategies to use in your classroom

- Reference note cards. These could be definitions of vocabulary words, a math formula, or a list of your lessons steps.
- Graphic organizers. Organizers arrange a paragraph to help your kids plan out their thoughts and ideas.

- Repeated reading. Every learner has his or her own speed in processing information. Reading the same text over again is giving the learner more time to practice.

- Partners. Match your student with a peer who has mastered the concept you are working on. Have the peer help teach your struggling students.

- Mini lessons. These are quick five-to-ten-minute lessons given after the main lesson. Take what you taught the whole class and modify it to match the struggling learners.

Putting it all together

Students need to feel successful. Hopefully, you have groups of four to six students separated by academic levels. These levels allow for students to work with peers and progress together as a team. Think about when you walk up a set of steps. It is easy to walk up one or two. It is very difficult to walk up three or four steps at a time. Without the foundation of each step, you cannot start building the structure on which the curriculum is based.

Grouping your students according to where they rank in the curriculum allows for mastery of a standard at each learner's current ability. Again think about each group starting at a different step. The teacher is differentiating the learning experience within these groups. From experience, I have learned to not move students on to the next level or group until they have mastered a skill. If the end-of-unit test shows they scored below 80 percent, you need to keep working on that skill with the group.

Groups keep your workload manageable. Schools are interested in how you have helped students improve academically per each level. You can only demonstrate this clearly with data and with a clear understanding of each student's academic baseline.

Model your lesson. Think about how the children can reproduce material from the end product of your example?

Sometimes you may need to reteach a lesson, and practice makes perfect. Create a mini lesson to reinforce a skill. What makes the true athletes really great? Practice. When I coteach or teach a small group lesson, often it is a review of the same material with a different modality or activity. Students are learning the same material in a different way.

When does a teacher transition groups to the next station? The timing is up to you, but the key is consistency. If you have three groups for one hour, then each group gets twenty minutes. Groups will move in a clockwise or counterclockwise fashion, moving to each center. Get a timer; use it daily.

If you are already rotating your groups to each center, introduce the new activity at the teacher-led center. When students come to your teacher-led table, teach them what to do. Teachers call this the I-do portion. Then, watch and see if the students can do it on their own. Teachers call this the we-do portion. Question the students. Use strategies such as ask students to finish your steps or supply the wrong answer and have students correct you. If some students understand the material, let them be the leaders at the center. If they did not grasp the concept, try to teach them another day at your teacher-led table. If they comprehend the center idea, let the group take it to their next center and work on their new task. Children can practice at the independent center completing the you-do portion. A good rule of thumb is to plan lessons by the I-do, we-do, and you-do model.

If you use free choice for students picking their centers, you might end up with students at all different academic levels sitting at the same center. Create packages for each group at each center. We will call this group the writing center. For example, a student placed in Group A can choose to start with a writing activity from the Group A folder. The student can read the directions and execute. Another student, from Group C, who wants to work at the writing center can open up Folder C and begin to write. Pupils from Groups A and C are at the writing center doing a similar activity at separate levels.

It's up to you as a teacher or parent to meet the student where he or she is at academically, building the steps to progress each student to a higher independent level. Creating lessons in which learners can succeed is the building block of teaching stamina to students. Stamina is the key to success.

As Einstein beautifully put it, "It's not that I am so smart. It's just that I stay with the problem longer."

What was Jesus's first name?

–Kindergartener

8

Freedom of Speech

Chase, better known as Michael Jackson, returns. The scene is my dreary dark closet converted into a classroom. Four students have been pulled out of their regular classrooms to join me in my palace of knowledge. These second graders have all been separated into different classes for the safety of the student body. I have the pleasure of teaching all the culprits in one tiny room. Minus the pleasure.

"For today's lesson, we are going to find our vowels in a word to determine if it's a long vowel or a short vowel."

"What is a vowel?" Michael Jackson says, shrugging his broad, indifferent shoulders.

My chin drops as if I have just seen a unicorn. By second grade, students should be able to identify a vowel. "Come and point to a vowel on the board," I demand in shock.

Excited to move, Mr. Jackson points to the letters: c, t, and e. Realizing that my lesson is totally in vain because this child cannot identify a vowel, I begin changing my plans by listing *a, e, i, o,* and *u* on the board. "With a few exceptions," I say, "vowels must be present in a word."

After two minutes, Michael starts singing "All the Single Ladies," by Beyoncé. My culprits begin to chuckle. I lose my reign as the leader over the classroom. Michael Jackson begins to shake his butt. This misbehavior is the reason he does not know his vowels in the first place. While this attention-seeking maniac might make a good co-median someday, he will never succeed without the ability to read a joke.

I issue a consequence to Chase, but the King of Pop does one last move, spinning 360 degrees to land gracefully on the ground in a breakdance position. I roll my eyes and then stare straight at his soul. Luckily, as a teacher, your stare becomes a weapon, and my eyes have the ability to turn to fire. This natural phenomenon comes when all patience is lost. It is one of those days when internally you are say-ing to yourself, *Either you listen to my directions, you little jerk, or my eyes will melt your organs. Your choice!* While you glare demently in his direction, everyone will stop laughing; they know the look and are now afraid of the consequences. Chase, seeing the look, simmers down, for he must be feeling his internal temperature rising.

With my right hand, I comb back my hair, a nervous tick I am devel-oping when I am angry. I regain my composure to address the class to say, "During this activity, we need to look for these vowels, *a, e, i, o, u,* and the sounds they make with other consonants."

My original intent was to have an activity where the students would kinetically move long and short-vowel cards. However, I always be-gin a lesson with a check for understanding question. This check is necessary in order to proceed with the lesson or in this case make some on-the-spot changes. Look at the simple difference an *e* does to a word. We will eat a hug pizza tonight. We will eat a huge pizza tonight. With any lesson, background knowledge must be known by the student to move forward.

The pupils would have to produce and spell the short or long vowel on an index card. Then move across the room and place it in the correct bucket. This was to respond to Michael's kinetic learning needs. Additionally, the students would be required to answer my question, how do you know it's a short or a long vowel? This check for understanding also develops higher-order thinking. All this planning, and then I see Mr. Jackson decide to invent a yoga pose, lying down on his back while his legs touch his head and his butt is in the air. He could lick his toes if his shoes were not on his feet.

"I'm looking right at you." As he stares at me between the gap between his legs, his butt is pointed in my direction, and I begin to feel my supernatural ability to produce fire beams shoot from my eyes.

No more nice teacher. I had two behavior management systems at the time. Way too many, and you should learn from my mistakes. We had a color chart indicating how each student was behaving. If you landed on red, you received a phone call home. I move his color to red with little reaction from my student. However, he ceases the yoga pose and sat up straight to listen.

"Let me tell you about our game," I shout, already exhausted five minutes into our lesson.

I start with modeling the I-do procedure. I choose a word from our weekly vocabulary word wall. I identify the word *kite* as having a long vowel, and I walk to the long-vowel box. For the we-do portion, students must prove their understanding of the short or long vowel. Before they can get up and place the word in the correct box, they have to check with me how they understand. Once they have completed their check for understanding (CFU), they can start doing the activity on their own.

My CFU question proves that Chase has trouble identifying the vowel sound in the word. He says *bit* instead of *bite*. I allow Mr. Jackson to watch the others to grasp the concept and have him wait as penance for giving me gray hairs. Michael's antics earlier in the lesson gave me reason to delay his gratification. Michael gets a turn and bursts forward to complete the activity. He proves that he can distinguish the short from the long vowel with his pronunciation and a CFU spelling the word. Everything seems to be going smoothly, but my luck runs out. I mistakenly turn my back for a second and out of the corner of my eye see a cartwheel.

I don't say anything; my eyes do all the talking. I make him wait. He perches himself on his knees, finally showing remorse. I give him his turn last, but before I grant his wish to participate, I ask, "Michael, do you owe me an apology?"

"Sorry." He looks apathetic.

He doesn't really mean it, so I continue, raising my voice, "For what?"

"For the cartwheel and putting my butt up and stuff," he mumbles with a sneer.

On the spot, I create a new idea for how Chase will participate.

"Chase, when you get up, I want you to skip until you get to the box where we sort our vowels. That way you can move more and get your energy out. I trust that this opportunity will not be in vain, and you will not dance, cartwheel, or make gestures to distract the class." I say with heart. I humble my heart, remembering that if I give Chase what he wants, he will give me what I want in return. All I want is for him to learn the material.

Perking up on the carpet, Michael says, "OK."

Did I mention I am being observed? This is my first year of teaching. My job is on the line, and every word of my lesson will be scrutinized after my principal's observation.

Would he say that MJ's rendition of "All the Single Ladies" was in key? Might I be moving back to my parents' basement?

I begin to rationalize and plan out the conversation my principal and I might have in the future. "See, we were actually talking about mating rituals of the birds of paradise in New Guinea. Yes, I do believe this was Chase's rendition of 'All the Single Birds' and their mating rituals."

My principal asks, "Why are you teaching mating rituals to second graders?"

With a big, overly enthusiastic smile, I say, "Who doesn't talk about birds of paradise in the second grade?" My eyes widen, searching for job security in his demeanor.

The patience on my principal's face diminishes, and he folds his arms.

Reluctantly, I say, "At least during this lesson everyone kept their clothes on. Yup, we are not bringing up peeping Toms in this school, no sir." I give him a firm pat on the shoulders, and I see no change in his expression. As I exit through the door, I reach into my pocket to call Mom to see if my room is still available in the basement.

Back to the lesson. The students begin writing on index cards and sorting out each word. Chase is jumping and understanding the phonics lesson, to my delight. We have a good conversation discussing how a vowel in a word like *tap* would say *ahh* and how a vowel in a word like *tape* would say *aaa*. Chase is catching on and enjoying the chance to move his body around our room. *Maybe I won't have to move back to the suburbs.*

My principal begins to nod and write down some positive notes, I hope. Chase bumps into another student, Trevor. Chase leaps on Trevor and places his hands around his neck. My principal stands up, worried. "I got this," I yell but think, *I don't got this.* I pull Chase off Trevor and gently point to the principal sitting in the back to awaken any mercy they might give me to stay on task to keep my job.

Chase calms down, making his way back to his seat. Trevor, the other culprit, is glaring at Chase.

"I got you good," Trevor says, grinning.

"Don't you dare get out of your seat," I yell at Chase as I see him motion to leap at Trevor.

"This fucking shit is stupid. I hate this crappy school."

"Chase! You can't cuss in school."

"Freedom of speech, motherfucker!"

I do not know what to say. I just say, "Whoa."

The principal rises and with a commanding voice declares, "I got the freedom to call your parents on a Monday, on a Tuesday, and today. I have the freedom to take away all the privileges you think you have at this school." Damn! Samuel L. Jackson is my principal. Tight!

The class is stunned. Everyone sits back on the carpet on the assigned spots.

Although Chase is restraining himself, he is still furious. I needed to soothe his temper.

"What would make you calm down?" I inquire, still rattled by my principal's yelling.

"I want to lie on my stomach with my feet in the air."

Knowing Chase, if I deny his request outright, I will not get him to produce any work. I suggest a compromise and hope the principal will not intervene.

"OK, Chase, if you lie on your stomach, will you participate without getting in any fights?" I plead, knowing my job might be on the line.

Mr. Jackson gets his wish, and I separate him from Trevor. I show him the first card.

"Point to the vowel," I say to Chase.

"*A* and it says *ahh*. The word is *cap*." Chase says reluctantly.

"Great! Now what if I put a silent *e* at the end of the word?"

"It would say *aaa*, like *cape*," he states with more emotion.

He continues bringing over cards. The blood rushes to his head, and I can see excitement coming back to our lesson. I give Chase some praise, and he seems content.

"I told you I know this shit," he says with a smirk.

I guess he does know this shit. At least it will be easy to explain the First Amendment to him in the future. Freedom of motherfucking speech.

Teaching Tool 8

Check for Understanding

Check for understanding questions serve two purposes: first, to determine whether the student understands the concept, allowing the teacher to proceed with the planned lesson or backpedal, filling in the prior knowledge so the student can master a concept, and second, to incorporate higher-order thinking.

When teachers leave check for understanding out of instruction, they often leave a set of students behind. Teachers may assume that since students are in the second grade, they already know their vowels. Never assume. Odds are you know which students are struggling in your classroom. Use CFU questions to target your lower learners during your lesson. Do not rely on your assumptions when planning a lesson.

When instructing my lesson, I usually have only two or three CFU questions planned because I have data that supports the need to make the lesson different for each learner. From my weekly end-of-unit tests, I have much of the information I need to plan two or more lessons on the same topic. However, reminders of what the class has been learning never hurt, and check for understanding questions will support the retention of the current subject.

I have noticed through the years that students who are exposed to the more advanced principles are more likely to apply the material when suitable. The CFU questions allow the teacher to add an extra support for the lower learners, while maintaining the rigor for the whole group. What I was never told, but quickly learned, is often you have to have multiple lessons ready. Either with the whole group or the class, this is the time to have your differentiated lesson ready.

My thought process for how I plan my CFU questions and essentially create two lessons

- Lesson Plans: Plan the original lesson you have in mind. Then create a second lesson targeting lower learners. Think about the strategies of how your targeted students learn best and the skills needed to master your original lesson. Is there a different activity the lower learners can perform to show they know the material? Do they just need a double dose of the lesson?

- Check for Understanding Questions: Write down the names of students you will call on when asking the CFU questions. Determine who will need the different lesson based upon current exit slips and data.

- Lesson 1: I have the original lesson planned.

- Lesson 2: My Differentiated Lesson. Expose students to the same content when introducing the lesson, but the steps to solving, scaffolding, or analyzing the problem are on each student's individual level. Additionally, some students could go over the prerequisite skill if they are not ready for the original lesson.

By now you might be wanting some examples of check for understanding questions. I have posted some common examples, and hopefully this will help you brainstorm your own check for understanding questions in your lesson plans.

- How do you know?
- Can you give me an example?
- Can you put it in your own words?
- Check a false answer. Four plus seven is ten, right? Student says, "No, it's eleven."
- Can you show the steps you took to solve your problem?

Check for understanding questions and higher-order-thinking questions go hand in hand. I would say the main difference is a CFU question puts the emphasis on checking for prior knowledge. It's a quick cognitive check to decide whether to proceed or pump the brakes. The higher-order thinking sections are to dive deep to challenge your students. I created questions using Bloom's pyramid that I typically use to ask higher order thinking and check for understanding questions. I am introducing the pyramid now so the reader can understand how many CFU and higher order thinking questions can overlap.

Bloom's Higher Order Thinking Pyramid With Adapted Questions

(Typically, I use CFU questions at the beginning of a lesson and higher order at the end.)

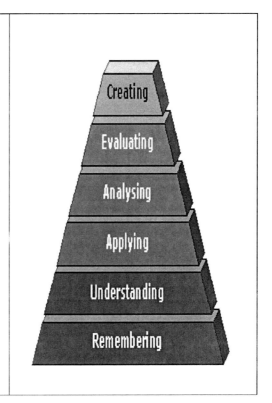

Creating
How can you develop your own ideas on this topic?
How could you do it different?
Can you create a new hypothesis?

Evaluating
Do you agree with the solution?
Could you compare/contrast?
Can you enhance the solution?

Analysing
How do you think?
What summary can you conclude?
What is the overarching idea?

Applying
Can you solve the problem?
Give another example?
Use details to explain your idea?

Understanding
How did that occur?
What might happen next?
Explain the main idea?

Remembering
Can you identify?
Recall the main details?
How did that happen?

Citation

Anderson and Krathwohl, A Taxonomy for Learning, Teaching, and Assessing: A Revision of Bloom's Taxonomy of Educational Objectives, Abridged Edition, 1st, copyright 2001. Printed and Electronically reproduced by permission of Pearson Education, Inc., Upper Saddle River, New Jersey.

If I was a lion, I would eat your corpse.
(a student learning about the lions of Africa)

–Kindergartener

9

She Fed Them Dog Food

It's Valentine's Day. Time to spread the love and appreciation to our friends. Time to make our friends edible treats.

Monique and Todd are always in a state of conflict. They play tricks on each other and may have liked each other in that awkward pre-adolescent way. Todd is the popular kid, seeking his acceptance by convincing peers to join his group. Students who refuse to do what Todd demands get bullied.

Monique is more of an introvert and a wanderer. She is constantly seen alone, sitting in a corner with colored pencils and sketchbook in hand. She is an artist. Monique stole school supplies and is brutally honest. Monique is not looking for social acceptance and is content doodling away during a lesson. Monique stands up to Todd and uses her superior intellect to plan her revenge this day. Beyond Todd, she really hates all her classmates, for they tease her daily.

The general education teacher and I decided to make a reward at the end of the unit. We said to bring in your favorite treat to share with the class on Valentine's Day. When the time finally comes, each student would distribute his or her treat to each classmate. Monique plays it cool and proudly presents her goodie bags to her peers.

Monique grins and tells the students that each bag contains Chocolate Puffs. You know, that delicious chocolate cereal that holds no nutritional value. From my estimate, she had put about fifty Chocolate Puffs in a sandwich-sized Valentine's Day bag with bright pink hearts. She wrapped each with care in a shiny red twist tie. Monique even has little notes on them saying, *You rock* or *You're awesome*. How sweet…

Monique has a reputation of trouble following her actions when she is not drawing in her sketchbook. Remember the penny incident? She watches intently as the children eat her treat.

Some say, "These are good," and continue to eat them.

Others say, "These are old," and choose to spit them out.

Todd says, "These taste weird," and begins to chew on them tentatively. However, seeing that others are spitting out the chocolate puffs only inspires Todd to chomp away more.

"How can you eat those?" a classmate says to Todd, only encouraging him to again place five more nuggets of love down his esophagus.

Out of nowhere, I see Brett run to the trash can and throw up. Next, Carla runs to the bathroom, and we hear the echoes of hurling. Then I see Todd; he clenches his stomach, trying to remain in control. Todd's complexion wanes to a yellowish tint. Pride comes before the fall as he pukes all over the floor in front of everyone.

Only one child smiles joyfully, Monique. The class locks eyes onto Monique as she tries to remain cool, but it's too late. She gives herself up by smiling. I have my first and only suspect.

"Monique, come here!" I yell.

I grab a bag of her treats off a student's desk. "What is in this bag?"

No smiles anymore. She refuses to tell me.

I say, "Well getting students sick is one thing, but getting a teacher sick? That is a worse penalty. My guess is you would never get to watch TV or play video games again for the rest of your life if you made a teacher sick." I reach into the bag and pull the "snack" toward my mouth. I have no intention of eating this poison but am calling her bluff.

"No!" she yells.

"Then what is this?" I demand.

"It's dog food," she says reluctantly.

"Dog food!" I scream. "Monique, that is pure evil. Do you realize that you might have poisoned your classmates? How can you live with yourself? What kind of person would give their classmates dog food?"

I quickly realize my reprimand had to wait; some students might have food poisoning.

"Show of hands: who ate Monique's treat?"

Thank God only four out of twenty students ate the dog food. One of the four students seems to be immune and continues eating a cupcake. He is the only one who did not throw up. The rest of the students spit it out because, well, it tastes like dog food.

I call the principal, and of course the principal responds by tearing Monique down. Then my colleague states that we should really call poison control.

We call poison control, and they tell us, "Well, we really can't tell you if it's poisonous until we know the ingredients or at least the brand of dog food."

Shit. I realize that I need to call not only Monique's mom about the incident but also the parents of the kids who ate the dog food.

I am thinking my conversation will go something like this: "Hi, Mrs. Smith. It's about Carla. Yeah, we had an incident…She ingested some dog food…No, there's not a dog at school…NO, we don't serve dog food at lunch."

I call down to the office to get Monique's mom's phone number. For about five minutes, Monique's mom rants, saying, "What? God have mercy! I am going to kill her!"

"Ma'am, I know we all want to punish Monique, but at the moment we really need to know the kind of dog food you have at home." I compel her to read me the ingredients. I quickly jot them down and the brand of dog food. With a heavy sigh, she tells me the name of the dog food, and I call poison control, again.

I have to explain the situation to a new operator, who says, "Damn that's messed up."

"Right, can you tell me if my students need to go to the emergency room?"

After five minutes of only the sounds of punching computer keys and an awkward silence, a nonreassuring operator says, "No, that dog food should be OK to digest."

Not thrilled at the prospect of calling the parents of the sick children, I ask my colleague to start calling parents, and I volunteer to talk to Monique. I go down to the principal's office to discover the true motives behind this evil deed.

Being a special education teacher means that when your students get in trouble, you often play the role of detective.

Monique is sitting in a chair in the corner of the principal's office when I arrive.

I witness Principal Laney on the phone with angry parents of ill children. He is trying to console each party the best he can but is just getting barraged with insults about poor school management.

I tell Monique, "You know, there are times when I have been really mad at someone or everyone. I just want to hit them. But I don't, because I know that hitting won't solve the problem. Then I realize I should tell an adult or the person I am having a problem with they are bugging me. It takes courage, but I know you have courage. Was someone bothering you? Bothering you enough that you would go through all this effort just to hurt someone?"

She nods her head in a sheepish fashion.

"Tell me who was bothering you and make me understand. Maybe that student needs to be punished."

Monique finally looks in my direction but not in my eyes. "Todd," she whispers.

"Todd? What could Todd have done for you to devise a plan to feed the whole class dog food?"

Struggling to say the words, she finally says, "He keeps teasing me, and he put a dead caterpillar in my desk, and it made me scream last week. The whole class made fun of me and the way I screamed. They are always making fun of me for drawing in my notebook."

I try to sound reassuring. "I was unaware that this happened. It took you a lot of time and effort to create something that would hurt everyone in your class. It shows great intelligence that you could hide your emotions from everyone. To not tell a single class-mate and to hide this plan from your parents show you are a smart kid. Is there anything else you don't like at school?"

"I don't like working in groups. I like working by myself."

"We can find a way you can work by yourself. If I can arrange this in your classroom, I want you to not act out in revenge when your classmates tease you. Do you promise?" I say sternly.

"Promise," she said, sitting up straight, her widening shoulders expressing that she was less anxious.

"What you did was evil. I can't save you from the consequences of this awful trick you played on Todd and your classmates." Standing up I slowly shake my head to display my dissatisfaction.

"I will find out if Todd was punished for putting the caterpillar in your desk." Monique smiles slightly in agreement.

"You realize, if you put forth this much time to your schoolwork, you would not have any trouble in school? Let's make a deal. First, I will make sure you are challenged in school, and second, I will never eat a dinner you have prepared."

She smiles, and we began building a relationship of trust.

Monique is suspended for three days, and Todd had been previously punished. The point is that I acknowledged Monique's side of the story. I made her realize I care about her feelings and learning. In order to make the positive changes in Monique's life, I need to be the good cop, the person to empathize with her mistakes and give her an opportunity to change her life. Plus, I personally want to increase the chances of a dog food–free learning environment for all.

Can we get a new teacher? You say no too much.

—Fourth grader

Teaching Tool 9

Higher-Order Thinking

I still can't believe that Monique fed her classmates dog food. Hopefully, she doesn't develop psychic powers and we don't have another Carrie on our hands.

My conclusion from this incident made me realize Monique's education needs to be personal, with the same creativity she gives her art. She needs to be truly challenged, because when Monique is off task, enemies are created. Monique is clearly an introvert who never raises her hand during small-group activities. Monique's boredom is evident, for when she does want to pay attention, she aces her test and spends the remainder of the time doodling. Monique enjoys when I ask a question of her directly. Questions that involve problem solving. It was time to challenge Monique.

When she returned from her suspension, I had her take another student survey. This time I added more open-ended questions, including "What activities would get you excited about coming to school?"

Monique's responses:

Finding information on the computer.

Make a project on a poster.

Work by myself or with only one friend.

I want to learn more about science.

How could I incorporate higher-order thinking into an independent project for Monique? If you refer back to the higher-order thinking pyramid in teaching tool eight, a teacher can start with any higher-order-thinking question. For Monique, I could have her analyze information on the computer, picking a topic of interest for her to work on. I could then have her make a poster of her findings. I was able to give her work a chance to shine.

Once we incorporated these strategies into her day, the teasing from her classmates seemed to diminish. Monique was occupied and engaged.

Monique had mentioned the computer on a previous survey, but I wrote it off because most kids want to play on the computer all day. I thought the allotted time every pupil received on the computer would satisfy her ambitions; I was wrong. Monique could be trusted to research and create a science project. I gave her the responsibility, and she began to own her education. What she wanted was to display beautiful art in an informational manner on a poster that was well planned. Sound like a similar kibble story you have heard of recently?

If you are thinking, *After that dog food stunt, she doesn't deserve anything*, then I ask you this: do you forgive people who hurt you? Forgiveness and trust are two entirely different concepts. I forgave Monique so that we could work out how to manage her behavior. I won't trust her when she bakes. It's quite comforting to hold on to the pain that someone inflicts on you, because it makes you feel in control. Anger serves as power over a person, and that person can no longer hurt you. However, you are going to have to learn to forgive and forget often as a teacher or parent. In fact, forgiving someone is the more honorable and healthy thing to do.

I am not a psychologist, but I do know that I have experienced freedom in letting anger go. Plus, we were going to go through the same experience with Monique again if the root of the problem was not discovered. Once I was clear on Monique's wants, I needed to use the same passion I saw in her art in other areas of her academics.

The following week I gave her a topic to research on two similar types of seabirds. I asked her to compare and contrast her research on a poster. My questions to her were: *What shows you that the male and female seabirds work together? Show me through illustrations how the males and females work together to build a nest? In your own words, which set of seabirds has a better plan for building the nest? Create your own seabird survival guide for a baby gull.*

This format for learning is based on a method of teaching called *project-based learning*, which is gaining steam in some school systems. By no means during my first years of teaching did I create an amazing project-based curriculum. However, it did allow for creativity and for Monique to express higher-order-thinking skills. She was able to compare and analyze two texts from the web to form concise information about the seabirds. Using this project-based learning platform, Monique was able to blossom academically.

The students left Monique alone to work on her projects. We did not see Todd or anyone distract her while on the computer. After a few weeks, I asked if she still wanted to do a project with one friend. After Monique began presenting her project to the class, her classmates asked about her ability to navigate the internet. One day she came to me to inquire, "Can Chloe and me do a project together?" Of course I said yes, and that was when I noticed Monique begin to smile at school. Monique was thrilled each day to be able to work by herself or with Chloe.

Monique's academics progress skyrocketed. She stopped sketching by herself during recess and was starting to make friends. The class did enjoy her biweekly projects, even Todd. Slowly she began to socialize and we rarely had any incidents involving teasing. By the end of the year, she had grown a year and a half academically. Remember, when building a unit, to create activities with higher-order-thinking skills. Refer back to the higher order thinking chart to spark ideas of how you will incorporate higher order thinking questions in your lesson. The troubled student might need the right kind of challenge.

I wish someone we knew would die
so my mommy and me could buy flowers.

—First grader

10
Gollum and His Precious

When one thinks about child tantrums, a vision of tears, pouting, and puffy eyes may come to mind. When I think of tantrums, I see books flying and my student transforming into Gollum from *Lord of the Rings*. He appears from a under a desk, hysterically saying, "I want my precious." My interpretation of tantrums may be different from yours. Gollum did not die with the ring in Mt. Mordor; he is a student in my classroom named Tyrone.

I remind Tyrone about our reward system. I can see the signs of a melt-down, as this question is intended to remind him to stay on task. My intention is to reward Tyrone if he gracefully lost a game. However, our academic board games do not suffice, and his thoughts dwell on something more precious.

Tyrone's obsession to win at every game leads to these tantrums. If he loses, we spend about five minutes cleaning up thrown school supplies. We are playing a game with one other classmate. Tyrone is losing, and beads of sweat are forming on his brow.

Often perching on his desk, he resembles the beginning stages of his tantrums a hunchback like creature. He cannot give any attention beyond his addiction. Addiction? A strong word to use for a nine-year-old. He was addicted to an eighteen-by-twelve-inch black box with powers to dilute any young mind. It's force is so strong that at this moment, our dusty cave-like classroom will no longer restrain Gollum.

"Tyrone, slow down, son. What is your precious?" I ask.

"Me needs it. Me wants it." Oblivious to the world beyond his precious, he sneers at the very question, the audacity I have to ask what the precious is. Whatever the precious is, I am worried.

"You can't control it. It must be destroyed," I yell.

The child is still stewing in his seat; an uncomfortable look stretches across his face. I am wondering what the child wants, but I assume Gollum is not telling me because the precious is unattainable at the moment.

Tyrone, who has summoned all the patience he can muster, slowly gives into the will of the precious. Dark clouds appear in the room, and the lights seem to dim. By this point, I understand my classroom is going to be destroyed, but I continue my questions, for I feel a breakthrough coming. *What is its hiding in its mind? What's Gollum thinking?*

I am wondering when he is going to start saying, "Gollum, Gollum." Cough, cough.

Again, I ask, "What is the precious?" Finally a red face stares at me, and then he flips a desk, clearly overwhelmed by the stress. Standing with his fists clenched by his sides, he yells:

"My…my…PLAYSTATION!

At this point, I realize I need to buy stock in Sony, and, yes, a nine-year-old can have an addiction.

I raise my voice. "You will not go outside until you clean your entire mess up and read with the teacher."

Stupid fat teacher. Doesn't he know I needs it? Doesn't he know I get what I wants? Tyrone sulks, trying to decide whether to obey.

Tyrone chooses to slowly circle me, looking for a weakness in my stance and my muscular six-pack of abs. Discovering that I have but one portly ab, Gollum charges my belly.

Bam!

With all his will, he hits me square in the gut and ungracefully rolls on the floor.

Tyrone looks up with a smile but finds me unmoved with an equal grin. This time he builds up more steam to run me down. I am around two hundred pounds, even more so around this holiday season. Tyrone is probably only sixty pounds. He has not had time to work out the math.

He chooses to strike again, this time with an outstretched arm to try and push me to the floor.

A second direct hit, and he falls on the ground.

Defeated, he does not smile.

I can see his mind desperately trying to problem solve. *What could I do to break down this teacher? I know: crying!* Tyrone delays his crying. Ten seconds later, I see tears. This delay was way too long to fool this teacher. It was his last ploy, a sad attempt to gain my sympathy.

"Stop crying. You are not hurt. You started crying after you stood up. Keep this up, and I will call your mom, come to your house, and throw that Playstation in the trash! It's your choice, not mine. What would be the better choice?" I say, rather harshly.

Finally, with his head held low, he scuffs the linoleum floor with his black shoes. Crying turns to pouting, and now the child looks like he is ready to comply.

Thinking back on the incident, I do not care that this sixty-pound kid charged me. What else would you do? Report the infraction and send him home. What do you think he would do all day? Play his Playstation? Yes, I was growing wiser to his frequent suspensions.

Tyrone cleans everything up and reluctantly drags his book to my table to read. I take a big step in controlling the power the precious Playstation has over Tyrone. The next day I tell mom we must take away the Playstation if Tyrone does not behave in school, she agrees. No tantrums occur for two straight weeks. What do you know? He can self-regulate.

I am told by the secretary that Principal Laney wants to observe the improving behavior of Tyrone. I feel I am starting to make progress with my little Gollum and am happy to have the upcoming observation. Principal Laney was noticing fewer visits from Tyrone to his office and more positive reports. However, my principal's words to me are "push his buttons when I come." He wants to see if Gollum has really changed.

I pick a game to play that involves chance and the rolling of a die. The players move their pieces on a square game board after reading their sight words (commonly used words in third-grade literature). The players make sentences with their words. It is a modified version of a board game to teach vocabulary. To win the game, you have to place the word correctly in a sentence, and the teacher has to determine that your sentence makes sense. This element of chance and my ability to judge each sentence give me the ability to "push his buttons" as necessary.

Tyrone roles a one with the die and grunts while mildly banging the carpet. We are sitting in a circle.

The beast is awaking. Not again. I try to ask a question for him to regain his composure. "Do we bang on the carpet when we feel frustrated? What other things can we do to calm down?"

Tyrone says, "Say, 'Good job,' or squeeze my bear."

His opponent roles a three; another primal grunt from Gollum. Signs of Gollum emerge. Tyrone's small, cotton-stuffed, stress-relieving teddy bear is squeezed tightly. I got the bear as a strategy from a kindergarten teacher who said it had worked for Tyrone in the past. It seems strange for a third grader, but I am giving the idea a shot this week.

Tyrone roles again, this time a two. Tyrone gets up and stomps one foot, three times on the floor, clearly angry.

Principal Laney calmly records the behavior. It's my time for the redirection to sell my behavior management to my principal.

I say, "Tyrone, remember, there are rules. Stay on your number, no mean words, no cussing or stomping of feet. I will be forced to not give you your free-choice time today. Time when you can play games and a positive report to Mom so that you can play Playstation at home.

Reluctantly, Tyrone returns to the carpet, pouting.

Three months ago, he would not have returned gracefully. Huge progress, as now the child can accomplish some self-correcting behavior.

His opponent roles a five, and I see the bear being choked.

Note to self: Don't have de-escalating devices that look like you're choking the living bejesus out of living things.

Now it is Tyrone's turn to roll. He rolls a one. "Fuck!" he yells. Realizing the enormity of his word, he covers his mouth in an attempt to suck up the syllable that hangs over the room, leaving all of us shaking our heads.

Fortunately for Tyrone, he looks remorseful and does not start his usual tantrum.

I ask slowly and take my time to deliberately convey the need for him to show remorse for breaking the rules, "Did you say the F-word?"

His opponent, not a fan of Tyrone, says, "I heard it. I heard the F-word!"

As a teacher, I find it takes all I have to restrain myself from smiling. His opponent's condemning confirmation of Tyrone using the F-bomb was priceless.

I witness the principal scribbling notes, and lucky for me, Tyrone sees Principal Laney's despondent expression. Tyrone's lips press tightly together. His upright stance wanes, and his arms fall heavy to his sides. He understands that he is in trouble, that the almighty Playstation might be taken away. Finally, he takes in a big breath. Tyrone says, "Sorry," the first true sign of repentance for Laney to record.

"I am glad you are sorry, but you did cuss. I have to tell mom your Playstation is gone for the night." Clearly sad, he takes the consequence and sits back down to finish the game.

Each opponent is one roll away from being victorious. Tyrone's opponent rolls a six and clearly will win. Tyrone grabs the mangled teddy bear by the neck and then grabs its head, compacting the bear into a small ball. I stand there contemplating. *I am surprised that bear still has a smile on its face.* Tyrone stands up, signaling he is going to kick the bear for a fifty-yard field goal.

I ask, "Is that the best choice?"

Tyrone stares directly at Principal Laney. He loses the grip around the Teddy Bear, and the bear appears to breathe a long-awaited breath.

Tyrone says, "I hate losing," but does not throw the bear, responding, "Good job," to his opponent. I see Principal Laney happily nodding recording the behavior. *Yes!* I have a record of an incident during a game when Tyrone did not have a tantrum and was able to regulate his emotions. My principal finally sees me improving as a teacher!

Tyrone says he is sorry because he knows I will follow through with my consequences. Once I found out his Playstation is his prized precious, I quickly had an agreement with Mom that any tantrum would render the Playstation obsolete for the night.

The consequence of losing his Playstation is too much to handle. In the past, I believe Tyrone never lost a board game, or if he did lose, his tantrums made you regret it. When I am around his mom, Tyrone seems to always win the argument.

I stand in front of Tyrone, proud of him for not having a full-blown tantrum. He is making progress. My new goal is to see Gollum only in a major motion picture.

We gather the pieces off the board and play another round. As I move across the room, watching my culprits play the game, I hear his opponent softly whisper, "Tyrone, maybe next time we play, you shouldn't say, 'Fuck.'"

Teaching Tool 10

Make Your Lessons Fun!

What makes your students motivated? We covered how to obtain students' interests from student surveys. Why did you choose to be a teacher or parent? Hopefully, you want to have fun with your children. A teacher or parents can take any lesson and make the activity fun. For example, maybe your students like music. Have you considered going online and finding songs that match your unit lesson? Reading song lyrics could energize your struggling learner to want to read.

Games are a great resource to use at centers and stations. By implementing a game at a center, you are keeping your pupils engaged. Plus, you can witness the joy that comes from playing a game rather than completing another boring worksheet. Personally, I learn best when I read on a subject I am interested in, and the same goes for those you are teaching.

It's not only my opinion that correlates academic gains and joy. There is growing sentiment within the educational community that schools are only catering to standardized tests. The bureaucracy favors the gains of test results, and we care less if our students are actually applying our concepts in the real world. We continue to push standardized testing, and the US school system continues to fall behind, compared with other developed nations. The irony behind this testing is that we spend more time than ever on the standardized testing that is supposed to show how intelligent our students have become.

Ms. Garfield was my sixth-grade teacher in middle school. We were learning about World War II. Instead of worksheets, we had an exhilarating assignment. The class broke up into groups according to what interests we had about the war. Each group would make a radio broadcast creating propaganda that supported a side in the conflict. I was interested in how the propaganda led Germans to believe in the lies of Hitler. I spent more time on that project than any assignment until college.

The time came to present our propaganda broadcast to our German citizens in the classroom. My group's radio broadcast relayed the evils of the Soviet Union and why we must invade Russia. During the summer of 1942, the Germans had reached Stalingrad in Russia. Our job was to boost morale because the German troops were beginning a stalemate with the Russians.

The German troops were supported by the *Luftwaffe*'s aerial bombings. The Luftwaffe was the aerial branch of Germany during World War II. We gave reports in our broadcast about how the Luftwaffe was necessary to win the war over Russia and asked mothers to sow blankets because winter was coming. Each broadcaster was allowed to have a radio voice. Mine sounded twangy, something out of the 1920s. The whole class listened intently to our information, and we refuted lies by the Allies over the broadcast. The class realized that since we were the only media source for the Germans, it would be easy for the German citizens to believe our broadcast.

Why do I remember Luftwaffe was the aerial branch of the German armed forces? Ms. Garfield made the radio broadcast fun and instilled in me a love of learning. It takes more upfront effort to plan a lesson the way she did. The teacher gave us criteria and the sources, but we gave back all the energy she put out to make that radio broadcast a great assignment. You will find the upfront effort is worth the reward. Our youth will conquer any curriculum we give them if we are able to instill a love of learning.

I have made an informal observation throughout the years. The professor or teacher who makes learning interesting and joyous is the teacher you remember, right? Smith, M. K. has similar feelings. Smith has written various research articles about how joy in the classroom directly relates to the knowledge the learner retains. Smith argues:

> All this poses a particular challenge to educators. Smith, M. K. (2005, 2013) comments, "Happiness and education are, properly, intimately connected. Happiness should be an aim of education, and a good education should contribute significantly to personal and collective happiness." Sadly, much schooling and non-formal education has become increasingly directed towards economic end. The result has been both a narrowing of educational experiences within schooling, and state-sponsored informal education and lifelong learning, and now, it seems, a sharply decreased ability to add to people's well-being. If those concerned with the "new science" of happiness are to be believed, much educational policy is profoundly misguided.

Beyond games, we need our youth to gain interest in the subjects they encounter. We need to allow for students to express their ideas through different avenues. Think about how you will let your students express their ideas. Think more about casting a wider net when you create a lesson. How are you making the educational experience fun?

The choice will be yours whether or not curiosity, perseverance, and wonder will be instilled in your classroom. Ms. Garfield's propaganda radio broadcast or the stellar star art project from your first-grade class, those are the events we remember from school. The teacher will have to decide if he or she is instilling a love of learning or pumping a student's brain with short-term test preparation to boost a school's statewide academic standing.

Motivating Students

We need to start giving students the responsibility and tools to handle challenges. We need to have a growth mindset and celebrate growth. This pass/fail culture of schools only leads to frustration. Give students enough time and the proper support, and they can achieve.

When teachers are having a difficult time with getting their students invested in their work, I ask if there is a culture of advocating self-efficiency. Are students able to monitor their growth? Are they given the opportunities to be responsible? Pupils want to grow up and prove that they are grown up. Everyone wants to be valued and respected. Giving someone the chance to feel valued and respected is a beautiful thing. Here are some critical questions you can ask yourself when thinking about motivating students.

- Does the student have some choice and any power over his or her learning?

- Do they believe their intellect is fixed and do they believe they can grow academically?

- Does the student feel loved and valued by adults around them?
- Does the child feel proficient about their learning?

If you answered no to any of these questions, then you probably have an apathetic learner. I take time to have private conferences with each of my students. I am uncovering the root of the problem of each student's apathy. Then I may ask questions like "Would you like me to post your science project on the wall for your parents to see on back-to-school night?" The student usually tells me if the parents won't show up or responds yes. I just discovered who needs a little more love in the classroom. I will make a larger effort to make learning interesting for that student.

Conferences are a great way to discover if my essential questions are being answered yes. Once you can motivate a child, then you make your lesson fun!

Tips for motivating in your classroom

- Individual responsibilities: Door holder, paper collector, pencil sharpener, and behavior monitor are some examples.

- Academic goals: Think of telethons when they are trying to raise a million dollars to help cure cancer. Some people give right away, and others wait until the last minute. However, collectively, everyone wants to reach the same goal. Have a chart where students mark their achievements. Reading an entire book for fifteen minutes, check. Writing a one-page informational piece stating the opinion and reasons to support your conclusion, check.

- Classroom culture: Show off exceptional work on a board.

Have students put Post-it notes on the work telling other students what they like about their peers' projects.

Citation

Smith, M. K. (2005, 2013). 'Happiness and education – theory, practice and possibility', the encyclopaedia of informal education. [http://infed.org/mobi/happiness-and-education-theory-practice-and-possibility/. Retrieved: Aug 9, 2014

DWECK, CAROL S. (1999) Self-theories : Their role in motivation, personality, and development. Taylor and Francis Group LLC Books. Retrieved: Aug 11, 2014

11
Reflections

If I were a recruiter for a school system and my stories were displayed on a poster, would you want to work for my school? Scantily clad children, kids feeding classmates dog food, and cussing nine-year-olds. Many administrators will not fully disclose the extent to which kids can behave in a school—partly for privacy reasons and partly to not scare away qualified candidates. I wrote this book for the teachers who have been thrown into chaos. To give you hope that you are not alone. In time, you can be more in-depth with your teaching strategies. If you feel you're up a creek without a paddle, use these strategies as a basic guide to survive your first years of teaching.

That's Special will be interpreted differently by each reader. A new teacher might be in the lion's den with unruly children, and this book could be a fun mental release. You might have a better behaved classroom and be thanking God that your class just needs some minor adjustments. You might be looking for a career change and asking yourself if teaching is worth it.

Many readers have asked me, "Dan, if teaching is extremely difficult, why choose this profession?" The pay is lousy, and everyone is against you. The students, parents, and administration will blame the teacher for any poor test results. Constantly, you spend more time on administrative tasks rather than actually teaching. Once you have experiences involving joy and challenges, you will make one of two choices. I could have a predictable desk job, in which everyone around me is in control of his or her emotions. Or I could choose to stay in education, to be an artistic force who creates captivating lessons that will mold society.

No pressure—you are a key factor for the advancement of the human race. Elementary skills are needed in almost every profession. Middle school and high school prerequisites are needed to be accepted into a college. It's much easier to correct emotional and academic deficits at an early age. Without your help, a student who does not have the tools to attend college and finish with a bachelor's degree will make on average one million dollars less over a lifetime than one who does finish college. Your words and actions will help propel students to be a success, or we could just give up to have more of our society on the welfare system. I vote for the first choice. The mission to educate is necessary, and few doubt the role teachers play in society, but do I (Dan) get satisfaction from being a teacher.

I experience joy on almost a daily basis. Being a teacher means fulfilling many roles. You will be a full-time counselor—who builds bonds of emotional stability to carry children through tough times. You will discipline them in an effort to create compassion and respect. You will push their minds to higher-order reasoning, increasing the mental capacity of the human brain. The teacher will motivate through challenges and to show remorse. Remember, it's tough love. Keep them alive and out of trouble. Make these young citizens realize there are rewards and consequences in life. There is nothing I have found in my life as rewarding as teaching minors the life lessons they need to succeed. Yes, it can get crazy, but in my opinion, it's better than a typical nine-to-five existence.

Teaching is an interesting profession, especially with students who refuse to fit the mold. I never grew up with the ambition to be a robot, and the same goes for our students. We should strive to create energetic learners with the intellectual capacity to seek multiple career options. We need to develop students who learn for the sake of learning, who are able to rise to the challenges, to overcome obstacles. Teaching is a public service in which we grow with the struggles of our youth.

Even at an early stage, I saw the potential of many of my students. I had to use my creativity to make multiple lessons for my students to express themselves. Plus, I had to meet my students where they were academically and fill in any gaps in their education. It's your job to help propel your students to the next step. I leave you with this one last story of how one little girl learned how to talk.

A witness to domestic violence, Takia watched her mom's body coil into a submissive ball as she was helplessly beaten to a pulp. This would happen anytime her mom talked back to her stepfather. From the accounts of the social worker, Takia slowly watched her mom become silent. Takia, afraid to speak anymore, would only silently shake her head yes or no to any question.

This nonverbal child entered kindergarten, and we educators had a problem. Everything inside us knew that Takia could speak. She could be seen laughing or crying if she got hurt, and by all accounts, doctors said her vocal chords were perfectly healthy. Her mom confirmed she was talking in full sentences a year prior. This silence was a learned behavior and a source of security. Our job as educators was to create a safe place for Takia to interact. More importantly, we needed to develop another learned behavior, courage.

"A puppet!" I said one day during our collaborative meeting. "Let's try giving Takia a puppet she can control to retell a story." For weeks, I was witnessing teachers in her face trying to force her to talk. How traumatizing that must have been for Takia, when all you know is that when you speak to an authoritative figure, you get hit.

With the puppet, the idea was Takia was in control of the situation. Performing plays was a way she could become another person and hopefully overcome some wounds from her past.

We gave three students puppets, and we modeled the lines we would say during our play. Then the three students got a chance to act out the stories. Takia watched intently as her peers laughed at many of the jokes inserted in the story.

For this particular play, everyone wanted to be Roger. Roger's one-liners would be silly, like "Jump a lump" or "That is rad." All Takia had to say was this one phrase: "That's smart like an aardvark!" We asked Takia to be in the play the second month of school, but she shook her head no. Three weeks went by, and with each passing week I saw her smile more at Roger. On a Monday, I asked for a show of hands for who wanted to be Roger. A half-raised hand appeared in the back; it was Takia.

The play was rehearsed while the other students were reading a story with my instructional aid. During her rehearsal, I said, "OK, Takia, your line is 'that's smart like an aardvark." I signaled for her to say the line.

"Smart like an aardvark," I say again, this time getting a nod yes.

"Smart like an aardvark," I said a third time while Takia stood there, silent.

I had to wrap up the rehearsal and hope for the best. The children said their lines while the students eagerly waited for Roger's character. Takia looked meek, downcast eyes stared at the floor, and then, gazing at her puppet, she grew a slight grin. Everyone stood in anticipation for Roger the puppet to say the silly one-liner. Takia looked away from Roger. Five seconds went by, then ten, then twenty. She blushed and swayed from side to side, her posture indicating she was uncomfortable.

A student in the front row said, "You can do it." Another said, "Say, 'That's smart like an aardvark.'"

Takia looked up and gave us a huge smile. Raising the puppet and with a deep breath, she said, "That's smart like an aardvark."

Everyone laughed.

In a moment of celebration, I picked up Takia and started dancing with her in the classroom.

Seeing my joy, everyone smushed together, hugging Takia in a big circle. The emotional stronghold that kept her silent was broken. I still see Takia years later; as far as I know, she is on grade level and talking with her peers. Who knew that the idea of a puppet could make someone petrified of talking speak? Who knew that as a teacher I could never feel more fulfilled?

Acknowledgments

Thanks for the wonderful memories, kiddos! I want to thank the many teachers and friends who gave me an opportunity to be creative. I want to thank my family for encouraging me to write these stories down and use my humor to teach a lesson. Any movie or play has conflict to make the story interesting. I often would flip through educational publications or scholarly journals revealing documented proof that students need movement in the classroom. I would say, "Well, of course! I know why they need to move—they're kids!"

Authors of educational journals have the best intentions. However, they have another set of skills: putting me to sleep. I prefer to relay information that not only educates but captivates. Just as teachers relay information to students through stories, I want to have stories teach the educator. Hence, I wanted to write a book for real teachers, with practical advice, that real people would want to read in their spare time.

Layered in all the ridiculous stories were real experiences you might encounter. It was not a theory. It was the product of inner-city pressures and many social dilemmas. We can't solve all the world's problems. We can each help a child in our community. We can laugh at their silly mistakes, and we can learn through our failures. Just as we teach our students to learn though their failures, new teachers can feel overwhelmed and need to know many teachers have had similar experiences. This book was intended to be a healthy emotional release of the heavy psychological burden placed on educators. Few people told me I would cry myself to sleep or admit that I failed. Yes, I failed and learned more through the challenges. Challenges are good; they help you grow. My hope is you can take a lesson from this book to improve your teaching or parenting.

I want to thank the teachers who encouraged my creative writing, who encouraged me when I struggled in my first years of teaching, and who supported me to try new ideas. I want to thank my wife and grandmother for teaching me to persevere. I did not need academic textbooks my first years of teaching—I needed a survival guide.

10 Percent to Charity

Ten percent of the profit from this book will go back to supporting local schools and organizations that support K–12 education. My hope is that you give this book as a gift to a teacher, parent, or friend who needs a laugh, and we can give money back to our desperately under-funded school systems. Thank you for your purchase and donation.

CPSIA information can be obtained
at www.ICGtesting.com
Printed in the USA
FFOW01n0052170715
15244FF

9 781478 752455